Sulayman Al Bassam

PETROL STATION

OBERON BOOKS
LONDON

WWW.OBERONBOOKS.COM

First published in 2017 by Oberon Books Ltd
521 Caledonian Road, London N7 9RH
Tel: +44 (0) 20 7607 3637 / Fax: +44 (0) 20 7607 3629
e-mail: info@oberonbooks.com
www.oberonbooks.com

A catalogue record for this book is available from the British Library.

PB ISBN: 9781786821492
E ISBN: 9781786821508

Cover image by Sulayman Al Bassam

Visit www.oberonbooks.com to read more about all our books and
to buy them. You will also find features, author interviews and news
of any author events, and you can sign up for e-newsletters so that
you're always first to hear about our new releases.

To My Children: Iskander and Noor

This play was written over a series of years. The first scenes were sketched at the time of the American led invasion/ liberation of Iraq, in 2003. As the wheels of war were turning again in the Gulf Arab region, I was reminded of the destruction that followed upon an earlier war when – in the aftermath of the Iraqi invasion of Kuwait in 1990 – the withdrawing Baathist Army set fire to the oil wells. The dust that swirled from under the incoming American tanks echoed the infernal landscape of burning oil, black skies and masked sun left by the withdrawing Iraqi Army, twelve years earlier. This is the black sky under which Petrol Station unfurls: it is the sky of more than one war, more than one violence. The character of the Bedoon (stateless Arab) is also a violence. One that afflicts several Arab countries in the Gulf and beyond. Questions of borders, oil, migrants, are not limited to the Arabian Gulf. The journey of the Girl opens this tale onto deeper histories and other wounds. Her journey explores imaginary horizons of the female voice; horizons not frozen in the static and self-annihilating maelstroms of religion and male sexuality.

The completion of the first draft was enabled by a residency at The Camargo Foundation, Cassis, France. Its evolution into final form was made possible by a residency part of the Visiting Global Faculty Programme at The Gallatin School of Individualised Study, New York University. My thanks to these institutions and to Professor Anupam Basu for his collaboration on the Bengali translation.

Foreword

With *Petrol Station*, Sulayman Al Bassam, the renowned Kuwaiti playwright, presents a powerful personal drama that is also a story on a global scale of migrants, statelessness, and the intersection of war, oil and profit. Set on the border between two unidentified Middle Eastern states, in a context of an unidentified war, the play speaks directly to contemporary political questions about refuges, immigration, war-profiteering and illegal border crossers. It features a leading character (the Cashier and son of the Owner and Ruler of the Station) who is a "national of the first degree"; a Trafficker or smuggler who is a dual national and can move across borders easily; and the Manager (an illegitimate son of the owner and a stateless person, born without papers or passport). A female refugee whom the trafficker has just taken across the border, explains that in doing so she lost her official nationality:

Girl: "I crossed the border and became stateless." The Manager responds, "Yours is a temporary affliction." This moment of brief humor highlights the fact that the Manager's own stateless state is permanent – he is a "blank," whose identity papers are left blank – he can never cross the border but must remain perilously within the boundaries of a state to which he also does not in fact belong.

Like plays by Beckett or Stoppard, *Petrol Station* tells its story of violence and near-apocalyptic destruction with a comic and ironic flare. Al Bassam's biting wit allows the play to be at once personal, entertaining and yet tragic in its larger political implications. *Petrol Station* is also tonally close to Brecht's *Mother Courage* in its dark representation of a seemingly endless war and the people who profit from it. "I love retreating armies. All sores and pustulence, skinned clean of righteousness. [They] Sell anything," says the Trafficker in good Brechtian form. And the wit is key: the Trafficker tells us: "I was a communist you know before I became a petrol smuggler and found God." And frustrated at how the internet keeps going off at the border – it has been out for many hours when the play begins – the Cashier exclaims: "No internet, no alcohol, war on the border.

I am going to have to turn to God." In addition to humor, the play also conveys a psychic devastation and quality of dark mystery like the endings of Sam Shepard's plays.

With these references to modern and contemporary classic dramatists, I hope to illuminate and locate in terms of the contemporary theater the significance of Al Bassam's achievement with this play. But *Petrol Station* also has strong Shakespearean overtones. Al Bassam became well-known across many parts of the world as he released starting in 2002 his adaptations or rethinkings of Shakespeare in *The Al-Hamlet Summit*, *Richard III: An Arab Tragedy*, and *The Speaker's Progress*, all three now published together as *The Arab Shakespeare Trilogy*. His distinctive voice – filled with wit, humor, irony and outrage – reshaped how many scholars and critics thought about the very plays by Shakespeare that his works responded to. His plays created an important, complex dialogue between his Arab Shakespeare and the Shakespearean originals which he uses as his inspiration and starting point, and in this way each work is cast in a new light by the other. Al Bassam made vivid through this lens the politically disabling effects of corruption, desire for power, and state-sponsored suppression of art and voice, and he brought into theaters and classrooms around the globe strong voices expressing the anger and potential violence such blockage has produced in a generalized Arab context. But he also made clear in each play that the causes of this political impasse lay as much with western and global power-politics as with specifically local leaders or governments, especially when the profits of the oil and energy industries and the selling of arms are taken into account. It is telling that the only entirely new character he adds to the cast of his *Al-Hamlet Summit* is the "Arms Dealer" who seduces both the corrupt government of Claudius but also the revolutionaries.

Petrol Station proceeds with a similar multilayered power. It is first of all a specific story that makes sense as an actual place: a petrol or "gas station" (in American English) near the border where everyone has to stop to get their tanks filled – armies, traffickers, smugglers and migrants, all trying to cross the border. Yet it is also a symbolic place, a picture of an oil kingdom itself, an entire state that is really just like a gas station, and in this aspect it incorporates the larger politics of the Middle East, including indirect references to the power of the oil industry, and direct references to the migrant laborers (often, as in this play, from South Asia) who perform most of the labor in the Gulf States. As Bayu, one of the migrant laborers (who speak Bengali to each other), puts it in a kind of mad-scene with Noah, a dying refugee (and brother of the Girl), who has been travelling in a leaky oil truck:

Bayu: My tribesmen are everywhere and everywhere put out. My tribesmen are hungry for change, not shy of blood, see wealth in the hands of the few and feel the might of the many…

Noah: Who are your tribesmen?

Bayu: "The pill bearers, the dirt carriers, the cement throwers, the garbage cleaners, the eyes gleaming in the pipes, the bodies in the burning tires, the sutures in the wound, Indians, Pakistanis, Nepalese, Koreans, Thais, the dark and yellow skinned… We the black armies of the black gold…"

Like this one, other seemingly straightforward political statements punctuate the story. We are given a biting comment on globalization in the contrast between the Cashier's fantasies of a future brought on by free trade and the Girl's demystifying of what it has really meant:

> **CASHIER:** "Commerce and free trade.
> The unhindered movement of goods and trade.
> The only true pillars of neighborly feeling,"
>
> **GIRL:** "Smuggle petrol into a war zone.
> Sell it to mercenaries to trade it
> for machetes to swing into the chests
> of children: commerce and free trade?"

And the Girl, a refugee who (through her own transformative inner journey) comes to stand for many women, maintains the hope that she can get out of the dark underworld represented by the Petrol Station and save her country from the brutalizing fallout of civil war:

GIRL: "I am out of my world, into another darker
nether world, but I am not lining up to join
the ranks of the dispossessed. I've a people
that need me, a country on the slaughter rack,
seized in the pains of a terrible becoming."

Yet for all the intensity of its political vision, the play does not provide answers – rather we hover on the edge of answers and solutions. Perhaps this is because the play itself hovers on the border between the brutally realistic and the symbolic. It focuses on borders, as non-places that call attention to the gaps and crevices in any notion of civilization that might reach to both sides of the border. The Trafficker, both a smuggler and a human trafficker, tries to claim that his "marriage certificate" for the Girl he has picked up is good on both sides of the border: "There are mores and customs, nephew, mores and customs; solid tangible rules, even out here on the edge of visibility." But this proves incorrect – there is no custom that rules at the border, and no solution for the writer either but what Al Bassam has his character, the Manager, call learning to "re-write" the world: "Watch name remember rename."

The play is set "on the edge of visibility" in many ways, then – a place easy to forget, that no one is paying attention to, it is also deeply polluted by war and burning oil. Anyone who has seen Sebastião Salgado's pictures of *Kuwait: A Desert on Fire* will be able to visualize the scene. As the Trafficker puts it early in the play, "who has ever seen black sky at dawn?" But the phrase echoes in a more existential and lyrical mode: we are "on the edge of visibility" in many senses. In this play we and the characters search for vision and even basic visibility, including the capacity to see and understand the meaning of this bleak border landscape and our own implication in these surroundings.

If the Petrol Station is both a literal place, a local petrol station, and an emblem of a petrol state dependent on the extraction of oil, it also has a third symbolic sense: it gives us the picture of life itself as sitting on a polluted border, darkened by clouds of oil fumes and smoke. A comic, apocalyptic tone reminiscent of both *Endgame* and *King Lear* pervades the play. As the migrant laborer Bayu says to his compatriot as they continue the senseless digging they have been assigned, "The signs of doomsday are gathering fast, Khan." It is a bleak humor like that which colors the heath scenes in *King Lear*: "the worst is not/So long as we can say 'This is the worst'" [Edgar on the heath] or "Is this the promised end?" "Or image of that horror?" [Kent and Edgar in response to King Lear with Cordelia's body] would be phrases perfectly at home in the final third of *Petrol Station*.

As the Manager is made to supervise the digging in an unbearable heat, he fantasizes about plans to leave – "A month from now I will not be where I am" and tells the Trafficker that "Our shadows… They're getting thinner." The Trafficker thinks this is sunstroke and hallucination, but the Manager insists, "The truth is approaching." But this is a question we remain asking: does truth approach? Or are we left with the choice of death, murder, escape (an exit) or explosive violence?

The plot turns on an order from the Father to uncover a lost "meter" used for measuring petrol. Joseph comments that "Father wants the meter found," and the following dialogue plays on the pretend surprise of the Trafficker, mimicking an inspector like *Casablanca's* Captain Renault of the line "I am shocked, shocked to find gambling happening in this establishment," but the twist of dialogue then takes us suddenly to a different space.

> **TRAFFICKER:** What's with the digging?
>
> **JOSEPH:** The meter, sir.
>
> **TRAFFICKER:** What meter?
>
> **JOSEPH:** Father wants the meter found, gave orders during the night.
>
> **TRAFFICKER:** What for?
>
> **JOSEPH:** Someone stealing from the station maybe, Father thinks.
>
> **TRAFFICKER:** No – that's terrible – Since when?
>
> **JOSEPH:** An inspector is coming to check the meter.

Yet the digging continues, and the unfound meter remains hidden, until the Manager, overseeing the migrant workers doing the digging, tells the Trafficker that he is "digging for truth." Eventually the Manager digs up not a meter but something altogether different – the past, remains of an unearthed corpse.

The "meter" had been given a larger significance at the opening of the play when the Father, after the call to prayer (as as an add-on to it) called forth: "My sons, when our Station began, it was founded on an agreement, a contract, a pledge. This pledge took the shape of the Meter. The Meter measures what is for us and against us. It is the substance of our bond with this nation; the record of our past; the guarantor of our future."

Like the station, the Meter is both a physical, literal part of the gas station, a measurer of how much Petrol has come in and out of the station, and an absurdist symbolic measurer of the very conditions of life in this border space. The meter can never be found and is never found, even as the station and the inheritance it represented blows up in the ending.

The final scene of *Petrol Station* is ironic about both ritual and rebellion, about both religion and politics. It begins with the four dead characters chanting in a choral ode the prelude to Islamic prayer, while the Cashier and the Trafficker half-fight over who will inherit the Petrol Station. As they blow up each other's half of the petrol, and the only inheritance that might have been is destroyed, they are left to end the play in a bleak apocalyptic comradery. They provide an epilogue like that of Shakespeare's Pistol who ends *Henry V* – "to England will I steal and there I'll steal" – promising to disguise himself as a wounded vet and thus to take advantage of the war. The Cashier and the Trafficker contemplate their future after blowing up the tanks of petrol:

> **TRAFFICKER:** What do we do now?
>
> **CASHIER:** Dunno. Register as unemployed?
> It is a rentier state, you know, provision
> for non-productive citizens is second to none.
> Had enough of being an entrepreneur.
>
> **TRAFFICKER:** And what about me?

CASHIER: We'll find you a mosque to preach in, day job, tide you over.

TRAFFICKER: I used to be a communist you know.

CASHIER: Don't brag. It's like saying I had polio. It's nothing to be proud of.

TRAFFICKER: We could join a militia.

CASHIER: Be no good, I'd kill everyone.

TRAFFICKING: Fucking Hell!

The play ends with them shouting "Fucking hell" together as the chanting of the Islamic prayer in choral form continues.

Petrol Station is not a tragedy though it is steeped in tragic loss and shaped by political blockage. Before the explosive ending, several characters – the Girl, Khan (one of the migrant laborers whose steals his confiscated passport in order to exit) and the stateless Manager – do manage to escape and to cross the border into a different space where there may be new options for agency. The play includes much not discussed in this introduction – songs, beautiful lyrics, the touch of desire and love. The play then is more than what the migrant laborers call it in their song: "A sketch of life in Petro-Dollar." It is that, but it is also a brilliant, dark, energetic and witty dramatization of the corruption of human motive, the failures of a domineering masculinity, the limits of an individual understanding of power, and the haunting of self and nation by our terrible interlocked histories.

by Susanne L Wofford

Dean, the Gallatin School of Individualized Study
and Professor of English, New York University

*Following a technical residency at Arts Emerson in Boston, **Petrol Station** made its World Premiere on the Eisenhower Stage of the Kennedy Center, Washington DC on March 24th 2017 in a production by SABAB Theatre with the following cast and company:*

Sulayman Al Bassam Playwright & Director

Cecil Blutcher	Noah
Kenneth De Abrew	Khan
Nasser Faris	Father
Christina Helena	Girl
Zachary Infante	Bayu
Galen Kane	Manager
Irungu Mutu	Joseph
Hardy Pinnell	Trafficker
John Skelley	Cashier
Hala Omran	Recorded voice of Mother
Eric Soyer	Set and Lighting Design
Sam Shalabi	Composer
Carlos J Soto	Costume Design
Brittany Anjou	Composer of "Cashier's Ballad"
Karin White	Props Design
Pamela Salling	Production Stage Manager
Lauren Stern	Assistant Stage Manager
Nick Schwartz-Hall	Producer
Rachel Katwan	Associate Producer
Ryan Gastelum	Production Manager
Frances Caperchi, Chandler Jez	Production Assistants
Deborah Brown	Casting Director
Blair Simmons	Social Media Coordinator
Nahed El Huni	Office Manager
Jack Llewellyn-Karski	Company Photographer
Alejandro Moreno	Spanish dialogue translator

Dramatis Personae

MASTERS

Father – the Station's founder;

Cashier – his son, a national;

Manager – his son, a Bedoon (stateless Arab);

Trafficker – the Cashier's maternal Uncle, a dual national;

Mother of the Cashier – a dead white woman;

MIGRANT WORKERS

Joseph – a Christian immigrant;

Bayu – a Muslim immigrant;

Khan – a Muslim immigrant;

Mother of the Manager – a dead black woman;

REFUGEES

Girl – a woman on the run;

Noah – her brother.

Note

The play is either bi or tri-lingual. The Masters speak their language, the Migrant Workers a patois version of the Masters' tongue and another language amongst themselves; the Refugees speak a different dialect of the masters' language, or their own.

Setting

A remote petrol station in proximity to a national border in the Arabian Gulf. Perched on the side of a two-lane highway, surrounded by arid desert, the station is dominated by a 1970's concrete canopy that provides shade to a tarmacked forecourt sheltering six fueling points on raised concrete plinths, a rudimentary air and oil point and an aluminum drinking water dispenser. Beyond the canopy, within the tarmacked area, is a cashier's booth. At the opposite corner: a single storey brick house with a minaret at the rear. In the upstage corner, a tumbledown shack roofed with corrugated iron and lavatories attached. Marking the perimeter of the tarmacked forecourt are accumulations of scrub bushes, remnants of plastic bags and old clothing snagged on half-buried coils of barbed wire. Beyond the perimeter, an abundant Cidra tree. The sky is tarnished, dirty and not clear. Tousled wisps and tufts of smoke rise on the distant horizon denoting, to the trained eye, 21st century urban warfare.

PRELUDE

FATHER: *(In the darkness, over the tannoy[1].)* In the name of
God, the Bounteous the Merciful and in the name of His
Prophet Peace Be Upon Him the follower of the right and true
path. My sons, my sons, my sons: when our Station began,
it was founded on an agreement, a contract, a pledge. This
pledge took the shape of the Meter. The Meter measures
what is for us and against us, it is the substance of our bond
with this nation; the record of our past, the guarantor of our
future. I had hoped that, over time, the Meter would become
ingrained in habit, etched into inclination, compounded
through action; that, in time, we would outgrow and shed the
physical necessity of the object and harness the Meter within
us like instinct, like conscience, like destiny: an invisible hand
that guides us. I was wrong. The Meter has been lost and
in its place, comes abuse and a fear that tatters sleep. Evil
has taken root in this Station; corruption, like cancer, has
seized its bones. Time takes us not forwards but as if a vortex
backwards, our purpose is forgotten; we know no longer who
we are. I am the falconer, but where are my falcons? My sons?
I have spoken. May Allah ward us from rumor and unproven
accusation: find the Meter, the bell of truth will toll. Long Live
the Station.

(Dawn prayers, called by the MANAGER, sound from the minaret.)

---

[1]Tannoy: Horn style speaker system used in public address systems

17

ACT ONE

SCENE ONE

Morning. Extreme Heat.

The CASHIER *is in his air-conditioned booth counting money in the form of banknotes and slightly oversized gold coins. Simultaneously, he makes repeated failed attempts to connect to the Internet through a laptop. On the wall, a U.S. Army poster showing the early and the later effects of cholera, malaria, and tuberculosis on human bodies. Hanging next to the* CASHIER's *head, a child's Superman figure dangles on the end of a string. The string leads out of the booth, linking to a thin iron wire that spans the forecourt and leads to the* FATHER's *room opposite. On the platform, the immigrant workers* BAYU *and* KHAN *sluggishly handle tools for digging. Overseeing them, the* MANAGER *stands thrashing bags of ice into a rusted metal bathtub. The door of the cabin opens. The air cleanser noisily pulverises dust. The* CASHIER *continues his failed attempts to connect to the internet.*

CASHIER: Fuck! Fuck!

(JOSEPH enters carrying a tray, covered with a cloth.)

JOSEPH: Eggs, master.

JOSEPH: Khan has asked to speak with you.

CASHIER: About what?

JOSEPH: His mother, sir, she's very sick.

CASHIER: Fuck! Fuck! This is not America.

(Enter MANAGER into CASHIER's air conditioned booth. The MANAGER stands in the doorway keeping the door open.)

CASHIER: Joy! Sing! Brother!

MANAGER: Give me some coins.

CASHIER: Close the door.

MANAGER: I counted the convoy, fifty trucks.

CASHIER: Close the door.

MANAGER: I saw you sucking one, it was so shiny and raw.

CASHIER: The coins belong to the nation and the nation bestows upon its children – of which you ain't one. 1959 Nationality Law: suck on that.

MANAGER: Sweating again?

CASHIER: O Bastard, bastard boy –

MANAGER: *(Pointing towards a figure on the transmittable diseases poster.)* You look like this one. *(Reads with difficulty.)* Cho-le-ra.

CASHIER: Close the door.

MANAGER: Been drinking from the taps again?

CASHIER: Close the door, you savage!

MANAGER: I've made an ice bath. You could join me on the bench. We could slap each other's thighs.

CASHIER: The bench is yours: the office is mine. The darkies are yours: the money is mine: each to his charge, we task-share the hardship post. Do we need drama? Do we need blood ties? Monkeys groom each other's fur of lice. We should do the same: exchange services. Despite the brutality of our surroundings, we could concoct an illusory, circumstantial kind of harmony. Close the oven door, I want to show you something. *(MANAGER steps inside and closes the door; the CASHIER opens a video file on his laptop.)* Had to flip through three proxy servers to download this minx.

MANAGER: Seen it.

CASHIER: Not this one.

MANAGER: Seen them all.

CASHIER: This is a collector's item: Uzbek. Showed it to your darkies, yanked their tails so hard, cum-pellets flew across the border like little acts of war.

MANAGER: Show.

CASHIER: Crash, fucking wholesale crash! Shithole! Wealth in every indicator, wealth in every bar graph and there's not a piece of anti-virus software that isn't pirated – even the U.S. army gear is pirated! Stay away from my eggs!

MANAGER: Think your little obscenities will buy darkie trust?

CASHIER: Fuck darkie trust. You extract their labour: I supply their leisure. You're Stalin, I'm Burger King!

MANAGER: Digging's started. Countdown's begun. Father wants the meter found.

CASHIER: I support that, bell of truth. Dong!

MANAGER: You're sweating.

CASHIER: I was the one that proposed that we install an integrated billing and inventory software management system; while bastard boy and your medieval bag of migrants are happy digging up the earth looking for glass dials I, the free man, am heavily future oriented.

MANAGER: Digging won't stop till they've found it.

CASHIER: They'll die of heat exhaustion before that.

MANAGER: Strong, man-muscle. *(BAYU lands a pick into the tar.)* Crack.

CASHIER: Then you'll be all alone, with your hands.

MANAGER: Split the face of the earth –

CASHIER: Ten fingered spade.

MANAGER: Dig into its bowels –

CASHIER: All bleeding knuckles.

MANAGER: Uncover the truth.

CASHIER: Plucking on your dick hair for hubris.

MANAGER: *(KHAN lands a pick into the tar.)* Crack!

CASHIER: I'll enjoy that.

MANAGER: The truth that breaks your back.

CASHIER: When you're not looking, they fill in the holes.

MANAGER: I'm always looking.

CASHIER: Pay you to watch them work: pay them to undo the work.

MANAGER: They obey only me.

CASHIER: Super-fucking efficient organisation. Should clone it.

MANAGER: When I find this meter, you might as well be dead.

CASHIER: Okay with me; get more sex. Isn't that why you pray?

MANAGER: The meter's your grave and my re-birth.

CASHIER: Your verbal intimidation is becoming more explicit –

MANAGER: Darkies want to knife you –

CASHIER: More frequent –

MANAGER: Tonight the knife!

CASHIER: I'll ring the bell!

MANAGER: You won't dare ring the bell. *(Pause. MANAGER eats from the plate of eggs.)* Need salt –

CASHIER: Underneath the ledger.

MANAGER: So do you.

CASHIER: Take and fuck off.

(MANAGER picks up a thin pack of banknotes from underneath the ledger.)

MANAGER: Tell your darkies to push in the whale, new head on it: Pump 5.

(MANAGER exits.)

CASHIER: *(Over tannoy.)* Joseph, send me my Uncle. *(CASHIER closes the door. To himself.)* Fuck fraternity. Fuck it.

Enter the petrol tanker in silence.

Sonically, we join NOAH's world: a cavernous, breathy, echoing world in which NOAH hunkers inside the dark cavern of the empty petrol tanker, strung out on Captagon, covered in grime, bleeding from an abdominal wound. He moans gently as hot drops of condensed petrol drip onto on his body.

NOAH: Captain, I can't see you, so listen well:
This belly is not the whale Jonah fabulously rode;
It is a pestilent void, dank and moist
Stinks of petrol, burns the skin:
A void you wouldn't put animals in for slaughter,
A void for broken migrants at best.
I think you are no sea captain but a ferryman
Of Dilmun or Hades on a chattel skiff
Humming with the visions of those who voyaged before me
That I'll render back to you
Through eyes dark as caves
In a cave dark as hell
On a day black as oil.

A bull with a monstrous member dances on its hinds,
At the teal green hour, shy of dawn
A village empties at gunpoint,
Women this side: men and boys that,
Gunmen up-lit with handheld halogens,
Labyrinths of teeth and antelope horns,
The infirm dig graves with their fingers
Children, agog, munch flies,
But there, quiet in the shade of a volcanic rock, a yellow snake uncoils.

My sister needs two pillows under her neck, not one!
The fumes weakened her, her chest is not good!
When she wakes, inform me, only she can read these dreams.

There's a hole in your boat, Captain, a void in a void,
Lucretius – banned in the Howza,
Hidden in pillows – Lucretius knew it well,
but the sea around us is dry as a kiln;
I think you are a sand shifter, a bone smuggler,
not a gold peddler, nor a treasure thief,
nor a man to be trusted at all.

The ridge is filling with the tyrant's men
I know from the pounding of their gaze
On your sun pinioned skiff;
sixty thousand eyes,
All looking to sever my head,
each iris an incoming mortar:
I know without seeing, but cannot see without knowing.

To your charge, Captain!
To the gardens of Kufa
Where the dates are ripe and the apples green,
There my followers await me.

Don't think to sell me on the way, peddler,
I lead the party of God,
God whose will is to sacrifice his favourites
On the oil dark day.

It ends badly only for me:
best keep your distance

Move fast, Captain!

SCENE TWO

(TRAFFICKER, smoking, walks towards the CASHIER's booth. He enters the air-conditioned booth; the air cleanser pulverises the dust.)

TRAFFICKER: I love withdrawing armies. All sores and pustulence, skinned clean of righteousness – sell anything. *(Pulling out a magazine.)* Take Sam North. Sam's mother was a porn star. Sam saw her in a magazine his friends were passing round in high school. Bomba: your mother's a whore and all your sticky fisted friends bear witness. Shock of it made Sam into a soldier. Killed more insurgents – men, women and brats – in twelve months than a bag of cluster bombs. But what to do? Sam's a broken man. Sold me the back edition he's been holding onto since his schoolboy days – his foundation stone. *(Handing him a magazine.)* Here, it's a gift.

CASHIER: Every time I see you, you get uglier.

TRAFFICKER: No! Every time you see me I get fatter – Allah be praised!

CASHIER: Joseph, tell them to hurry up, the old man doesn't sleep long in the mornings.

TRAFFICKER: The sleep of angels. I sympathise for you, nephew; an educated young man forced onto the filthy fringes of humanity. How's the model village coming along?

CASHIER: It's a city.

TRAFFICKER: Ambition! Admirable. I want a partner's share in all of this – *(Lifts the sheet on the model village.)*

CASHIER: Don't touch it.

TRAFFICKER: Yep. Having a degree from the United States of America – mighty useful for a smuggler.

CASHIER: Put out your cigarette.

TRAFFICKER: It's progress and I'm proud of you.

CASHIER: This is a petrol station!

(TRAFFICKER throws cigarette out of the window onto the platform.)

CASHIER: Shit!

TRAFFICKER: *(TRAFFICKER laughs and seizes the CASHIER's plate of eggs.)* Scrambled eggs! *(Eating.)*

CASHIER: They're battery. Hormone ridden.

TRAFFICKER: Put breasts on my hair! What's the matter, nephew? Need to fuck?

CASHIER: 72 hours, no internet. I've got the shakes.

TRAFFICKER: Bah! Internet!

CASHIER: Where's the booze?

TRAFFICKER: Come with me across the border and I'll give you the real girls, slippery tits and rock-tight pussy –

CASHIER: And a bag of clap.

TRAFFICKER: Clap-ity clap.

CASHIER: Stop frigging spitting egg onto my city!

TRAFFICKER: Nature's not clement in this part of the world, nephew, look at the sky – who's ever seen black sky at dawn – need to consider that in your design.

CASHIER: Just leave it alone.

TRAFFICKER: Tried blowing your nose lately? *(Blows his nose into a handkerchief.).*

CASHIER: Where's the alcohol?

TRAFFICKER: *(Showing the handkerchief to CASHIER.)* That is life threatening.

CASHIER: For fuck's sake.

TRAFFICKER: Security. Invest in security. We live unmoored by injustice, nephew, no surprise that violence grows upon us like facial hair. Ha! Joseph!

JOSEPH: Yes, sir?

TRAFFICKER: What's with the digging?

JOSEPH: The meter, sir.

TRAFFICKER: What meter?

JOSEPH: Father wants the meter found, gave orders during the night.

TRAFFICKER: What for?

JOSEPH: Someone stealing from the Station maybe Father thinks.

TRAFFICKER: No – that's terrible – since when?

JOSEPH: Inspector's coming to check the meter. Got a letter. Last time that happened was ten years ago.

TRAFFICKER: Hmm. So, where is the meter?

JOSEPH: By Pump 3's what I remember.

CASHIER: And?

JOSEPH shrugs.

TRAFFICKER: *(Seeing the MANAGER shouting at the workers and taking up tools himself to dig the earth.)* Made someone perky.

CASHIER: Fucking Bedoon! Thinks it's a call to Divine War, fancies himself God's chosen warrior.

TRAFFICKER: Where's the meter?

CASHIER: Who knows, no one can remember.

TRAFFICKER: *(Looking at JOSEPH.)* Not good news, nephew.

CASHIER: Neither are you. Joseph's taking care of it.

TRAFFICKER: You sure?

JOSEPH: I will, sir.

CASHIER: Yes you will, Joseph.

TRAFFICKER: Lucky man, Joseph.

JOSEPH: Why, sir?

TRAFFICKER: Know a lot and still alive.

JOSEPH: Anything else?

TRAFFICKER: Christian, too, aren't you?

CASHIER: That's all Joseph. *(JOSEPH exits.)* Where's the alcohol?

TRAFFICKER: Cleared me out at the border. Bastard new boss from a tribe I'd never heard of. Piss. That was his name 'Piss'. How am I supposed to swap favours with a man called Piss? From a tribe I've never heard of? Piss offended me. Piss won't last long.

CASHIER: No internet, no alcohol, war on the border – I'm going to have to turn to God. Fucking fuck.

(A veiled woman gets out of the truck and stands on the tarmac.)

CASHIER: Who is she?

TRAFFICKER: Who?

CASHIER: Trafficking humans now, are we?

TRAFFICKER: She needed a lift.

CASHIER: I don't like it, Abu Ghraib.

TRAFFICKER: Owed her family a favour.

CASHIER: People are messy.

TRAFFICKER: She's fine.

CASHIER: Get rid of her.

TRAFFICKER: Can't.

CASHIER: What?

TRAFFICKER: You know I've always said to myself; Bambooty, one day you will ask for the hand of a beautiful girl and you won't be refused because you are not scum.

CASHIER: But that's what you are: scum.

TRAFFICKER: Whatever your appearance, however pock-marked and stained, however many phials of excrement fate has doused you in, you will not be refused because you'll be rich and your wealth will annihilate the disgraceful odour of phlegm in your blood. She's my wife, nephew. My porcelain doll, wrapped in crepe paper. Here's your money.

CASHIER: Why d'you bring her?

TRAFFICKER: For the border, easier with her in the cabin.

CASHIER: I want to see it.

TRAFFICKER: What?

CASHIER: Her face.

TRAFFICKER: I'd sooner show my jewels to Jo Jo.

CASHIER: I'll see it.

TRAFFICKER: There are mores and customs, nephew, mores and customs; solid, tangible rules even out here on the edge of visibility.

CASHIER: I'll see her face or you won't fill the tank.

TRAFFICKER: That tank is a family bond, boy, if my benzene burns, so does yours.

CASHIER: I'm not saying you should leave me alone with her, Uncle, or let me do something to her that may warp her impression of our family.

TRAFFICKER: Like?

CASHIER: Play with her hair, dislocate a button.

TRAFFICKER: America's ruined you. I warned your mother. Look at you: all notions of honour, family feeling and respect built up over centuries, blown. Think everything's for sale? Stick a coin in your crack.

CASHIER: You're delicate natured scum, Uncle; I'm not suggesting we should not be partners. That we help each other crawl out of the lice pod, that's obvious, that I've already helped you lavishly, that's clear. But when we say 'partners' and what profit comes to you does not come to me, that's not so obvious, not so clear.

TRAFFICKER: Count your money – we're square.

CASHIER: I'm not suggesting you've robbed me.

TRAFFICKER: The border costs.

CASHIER: I know what the border costs –

TRAFFICKER: There are two sides and lots of fingers.

CASHIER: Just as you know what the darkies cost –

TRAFFICKER: Fat, poking fingers –

CASHIER: The half-blood brother, the sleeping father –

TRAFFICKER: The border comes out of my costs.

CASHIER: And I know what's missing.

TRAFFICKER: There's nothing missing.

CASHIER: And what you've – let's not say 'taken'; stick to banking lingo – say what you've, 'rented against collateral' is what's missing here –

TRAFFICKER: That's your share!

CASHIER: And that is how much she cost you –

TRAFFICKER: Count it again –

CASHIER: And therefore she's owed to me.

TRAFFICKER: I'll count it, watch –

CASHIER: If you want me to be your banker, then I'll be fucking Islamic!

TRAFFICKER: Don't shout! Okay. No. Yes. Whatever. N'ha. I paid for her in gold.

CASHIER: I own half.

TRAFFICKER: Seeing her face is more than half.

CASHIER: Which half? Which half? You poor, ugly, trafficking Uncle Scum; which half? Half the face, half the body, the upper half, or the lower half: the front side or the back side – your wife or not: I'm your banker and I decide. Otherwise, it was not a rental proposal and you were trying to rob me at sunrise in full view of my world?

TRAFFICKER: Who said you couldn't decide? We're family, why should I care?

CASHIER: *(To JOSEPH, over the tannoy.)* Joseph, bring your Uncle some chai.

TRAFFICKER: But gold costs more than petrol.

CASHIER: We'll split the difference. *(Handing him the porn magazine.)* I won't be needing this.

TRAFFICKER: Girl's a thoroughbred; keep it.

SCENE THREE

GIRL: *(By the truck singing a lullaby quietly to the tank.)*
Little dove send word to my love
Who went to Mecca to bring me a dress
To lay in my box.
Tell my love the key is lost,
It needs the smith
But the smith needs money
And the money's with the bride
And the bride has a boy

And the boy needs milk
And the milk's with the cow
And the cow needs grass
And the grass is on the hill
And the hill needs rain
And rain is in the hands of God. La Illaha Illa Allah, La Illaha
Illa Allah –
I know you are there, what do you want?

(MANAGER emerges from behind the truck.)

MANAGER: To love you.

GIRL: Got a car?

MANAGER: No.

GIRL: Money?

MANAGER: No.

GIRL: Passport?

MANAGER: Yes.

GIRL: What kind?

MANAGER: …

GIRL: Then, like I said, you are nothing.

MANAGER: I am not nothing because I want to love you.

GIRL: Because you are nothing you want everything, that's
normal. The world is full of your types.

MANAGER: You're too young to know what the world is full of.

GIRL: I'm not so young.

MANAGER: You are too stupid.

GIRL: Not so stupid not to know your type is only trouble to a
beautiful girl like me.

MANAGER: Who said you were beautiful?

GIRL: None of your business.

MANAGER: I don't believe you.

GIRL: Believe what you like.

MANAGER: If you were so beautiful you wouldn't hide your face in a sack, only ugliness becomes a sack. I may be nothing but I know what beauty is.

GIRL: How do you know what beauty is?

MANAGER: Because I rise when the rocks turn pink, conjure demons with my fingers and can incant words enough to make the night fall from your shoulders and the sun break from your waist.

GIRL: Shut up! You sound like a loafer and a thug and all these words just because…

MANAGER: Because?

GIRL: You want to rub your eyes over my face, and then –

MANAGER: And then?

GIRL: Then I don't know what.

(A feral sound of grating comes from inside the truck. The woman is tense; the MANAGER reads this.)

MANAGER: I'm not suggesting that you love me, nor am I trying to coax you into an act of love while they drink tea, but you are the one who called me out of the dark morning: you are the one looking for something, or hiding something.

GIRL: You were lurking behind the tires like a murderer. Leave now, before I shout for help.

MANAGER: I'm the Manager of this station and it's my duty to know what you are hiding. Will you tell me?

GIRL: Nothing.

MANAGER: Shall I shout for the truck driver? Yes, let's ask him. *(Calling.)* Abu Ghraib?

GIRL: Don't shout, please.

MANAGER: I have to shout, the sky is black and we can't see clearly. Abu Ghraib!

(She turns around, giving her back to the CASHIER's office and lifts her veil.)

GIRL: Look at my face! Look!

MANAGER: *(Mumbling.)* Oh my eyes, treacherous eye – tab my heart like this.

GIRL: I have your secret you have mine.

MANAGER: What secret?

GIRL: I saw your eyes widen when you saw my face. I see your need as clearly as you see mine. I know what I'm offering, you know what you are getting; you've had a down payment – no more need to talk about love.

MANAGER: No more need to talk about love.

TRAFFICKER *(Calling her.)*: Hafsa! Hafsa?

MANAGER: *(Giving her a knife.)* Keep this.

GIRL: What for?

MANAGER: Hide it. Hafsa.

GIRL: No, Aisha. My name is Aisha.

(MANAGER withdraws. GIRL, to herself.)

GIRL: Open up, doorman, open up:
Alone with my vulva, my beautiful vulva,
I'm all alone and I want to come in!

SCENE FOUR

[2]**BAYU:** হাত চালা, মোটু

[3]**KHAN:** কতক্ষন, বায়ু ?

[4]**BAYU:** যতক্ষণ না জাহান্নুমের দরজা খুঁজে পাস ।

[5]**KHAN:** Astaghfir Allah.

[6]**BAYU:** আমরা খুব কাছাকাছি – আমি বুঝতে পারছি। সব জিনগুলো এবার ছাড়া পাবে ।

[7]**KHAN:** Astaghfir Allah.

[8]**BAYU:** তুই খুঁড়তে থাক । সবকিছুর ব্যবস্থা করে রেখেছি । তারপর দেখবি এখানে কত কি পাল্টে যাবে

[9]**KHAN:** কি পাল্টাবে ?

[10]**BAYU:** নতুন এয়ার-কন্ডিশন।

[11]**KHAN:** কে বলল ?

[12]**BAYU:** ভিসার খরচ, আর বকেয়া ময়না ।

---

[2]BAYU: Keep digging, fat boy.

[3]KHAN: How long for, Bayu?

[4]BAYU: Till you find the find the gates of hell!

[5]KHAN: Astagfir Allah.

[6]BAYU: We're getting closer I can smell it, then all the jinn will be let loose.

[7]KHAN: Astagfir Allah.

[8]BAYU: Keep going dumpling, I've got it all arranged. Then you'll see some changes round here.

[9]KHAN: Like what?

[10]BAYU: New air-conditioning.

[11]KHAN: Who said?

[12]BAYU: Visa costs and back pay.

¹³**KHAN:** সব্প্ন দেখছিস !

¹⁴**BAYU:** মোটা, খুঁড়তে থাকে আর আল্লার উপর ভরসা রাখ।

¹⁵**KHAN:** এক বছর হয়ে গেল – কোন মায়না নেই। মাকে লিখতে সাহস হয় না। টেপ পাঠিয়ে চলেছে, শুনতে পারি না আর – বুক ফেটে যায়। মা ভেবে নিয়েছে আমি বোধহয় বেঁচে নেই।

¹⁶**BAYU:** মাকে লেখ তাহলে। *(BAYU sits down and begins to play quiet phrases on an Indian flute.)*

¹⁷**KHAN:** কি বলব?

¹⁸**BAYU:** *(He sings.)* পিরয় মা, এই হল পেটেরা-ডলারের জীবনের ছবি – কাজ কম, রোদ কম, মশা ও মালিক দুইই দয়ালু।

¹⁹**KHAN:** ভরা পেট, পায়ে চটি। মালিকেরা জ্বালায় না।

²⁰**BAYU:** ২০ জন চাকর ভিসায়। ১৮ নম্বরটা গাধা

আমি ১৭ নম্বর। যেন খাস রাজপুত্তুর।

---

¹³KHAN: You're dreaming.

¹⁴BAYU: Dig fatty and believe in Allah.

¹⁵KHAN: One year now, no pay. I daren't write to mother,
 she keeps sending tapes, can't listen to them anymore,
 they rip my heart into ribbons, she's convinced I'm dead.

¹⁶BAYU: Write to her then. *(BAYU sits down and begins to play quiet phrases on an Indian flute.)*

¹⁷KHAN: And say what?

¹⁸BAYU: *(He sings.)* Hello Mama, precious Mama
 a sketch of life in Petro-Dollar:
 Work is light and sun is cool,
 Mosquito gentle, boss not cruel…

¹⁹KHAN: Tummy full and toe have sandal
 Slave traders on me no handle.

²⁰BAYU: Visa 20 houseboy only,
 18 is the worker fool,
 Me I'm number 17
 A special one, a princely thing.

²¹KHAN: ময়না এতো যে তারে যাবে না, জাহাজ লাগবে।
শিগগির তোমার কাছে যাবে
যেন নবান্নের চাঁদ ।

²²BAYU & KHAN: দুধ, মধু আর তিল – নেই ঘাম, নেই শ্রম, নেই
কটু কথা

²³BAYU: এই দেখো ছবি: হামদিল্লাহ – ইটা আমি মক্কায়, হজে ।
মেয়েটিকে দেখ – কেমন মিষ্টি দেখতে। ওকে আমি বিয়ে করব,
দেখো – আমাদের বাচ্ছা হবে। তুমি দেখো, মা।
সমুদ্রের দিকে চেয়ে দেখি । ...

²⁶KHAN: সত্যি বলছি মা, জান্নাতের আরশোলারাও

²⁷BAYU: সুখের দাবি কিছু কম রাখে না। ..

²⁸KHAN: আমার বা ওর থেকে...

²⁹BAYU: আমার বা ওর থেকে।

---

²¹KHAN: Pay check too fat for Western Union
  To send you them I'd need a boat,
  And soon it will towards you float
  Fatter than the harvest moon

²²BAYU & KHAN: Milk, honey and sesame,
  No sweat, no toil, no acrimony...

²³BAYU: See this photo: Hamdillah,
  That's me in Mecca, me on Hajj,
  Now see my little Bālikā²⁴ (Girl in Bengali)
  She's hot and very Kumari²⁵ (Virgin in Bengali)
  One day I will marry her
  Permission pending pregnancy.
  Mama, Mama, I look, I look
  I look onto the sea...

²⁶KHAN: And safely say to you Mammi
  That cockroaches in paradise...

²⁷BAYU: Have no less claim to happiness...

²⁸KHAN: Than he, nor me...

²⁹BAYU: Than he, nor me!

(Enter, separately, the TRAFFICKER *and the* MANAGER.*)*

MANAGER: *(Shouting.)* Bayu! If I see your lips moving again in daylight hours I cut your water, 131 degrees and still no water. Suck on the black air. Keep digging!

(The TRAFFICKER *fills the belly of the petrol tanker.)*

TRAFFICKER: Busy?

MANAGER: Night and day.

TRAFFICKER: Renovations?

MANAGER: Truth.

TRAFFICKER: What's that?

MANAGER: Digging for truth.

TRAFFICKER: Only truth I know is the grave.

MANAGER: That's what this is: the grave of all the liars, traitors and hypocrites.

TRAFFICKER: Big hole, then.

MANAGER: No bigger than my hand; it's a cup that holds all the secrets.

TRAFFICKER: The meter! The Book of Judgement! I seem to remember it was in that corner, not over this side, why you digging on this –

MANAGER: Where's my passport?

TRAFFICKER: I'll give you a passport, for nothing, for love. It's shameful that you, our very own boy been left to grow into a man of undetermined nationality, a Bedoon, looked down on by the Banglas, cussed by the local girls. Who can tolerate it?

MANAGER: What you after?

TRAFFICKER: Justice! I'm going to get us a meeting with the Minister of Interior. Just you wait, now tell those boys to pack up their tools for the day, it's too filthy to work outdoors, let's share a cool Seven Up.

MANAGER: *(To TRAFFICKER.)* Keep the passport. I don't need it anymore.

TRAFFICKER: Anything you want within a month: Colombian, Bulgarian, Thai, no more of the third-rate Cambodia, Liberia shit.

MANAGER: I don't want the passport.

(Over the tannoy, "Mawtani" an Arab Nationalist Anthem from the 50s.)

Now what? Do we jog on the spot?

MANAGER: It's a lullaby, to keep the old man asleep.

TRAFFICKER: Your brother's not honest.

MANAGER: Runs in the family.

TRAFFICKER: It kills me to see that Yankee educated infidel sweaty – fisting his model village, flicking through porn in his air-conditioned cabin and you out here swarming in sweat like a beast. I was a communist you know, before I became a petrol smuggler and found God.

MANAGER: This is my lot: that's his.

TRAFFICKER: He's a profligate: you are noble. He's a cockroach: you are a stallion. It's a crime against nature!

MANAGER: It's fate. Out of my way.

The GIRL stands by the tanker and discretely moves to close the filling valve. We rejoin NOAH's sonic world.

NOAH: One, two,
Which part is true;
Three, Four,
They broke our door;
Five, Six;
Captagon fix,
Seven, eight,
Hell's high Gate;
Nine, ten,
Dead man in a pan.

(NOAH's sound world dissipates.)

MANAGER: Who's the girl?

TRAFFICKER: Flesh on the run.

MANAGER: Where's she from?

TRAFFICKER: Good stock. Political connections, you know.

MANAGER: What kind of connections?

TRAFFICKER: How much does that Yankee pay you for this?

MANAGER: What?

TRAFFICKER: Our game. The night game, the dawn game: what's your share?

MANAGER: I don't take from your game.

CASHIER: *(Over tannoy.)* Khan requested a meeting with the Cashier! The Cashier is waiting, Khan.

KHAN lays down his tools and heads towards the CASHIER's cabin.

MANAGER: A month from now, I will not be where I am.

TRAFFICKER: Don't tell me: Canada.

MANAGER: I'm already gone and when I'm done you won't be who you are either.

TRAFFICKER: I'm a new man, already: marriage does wonders.

MANAGER: Our shadows, Bambooty[30], our shadows.

TRAFFICKER: What about them?

MANAGER: They're getting thinner.

TRAFFICKER: Sunstroke?

---

[30]Bambooty: a smuggler, Kuwait / Iraqi / Ihwazi slang

MANAGER: The truth is approaching!

TRAFFICKER: Boy! Bring Mem-sab water.

MANAGER: *(Grasping the TRAFFICKER violently by the head.)*
Your eyes are plugholes, leeching truth out of my ditch. Away
from my digging, away from my ditch!

TRAFFICKER: Standing in the filth of day with a dirty, mad
Bedoon: now that's an honour that's hard to refuse but, if you
don't mind, I'll take my carcass elsewhere. In any case, I don't
want my guest exposed to cock breath and darkie screeching,
this is my honeymoon!

MANAGER: Tell her to keep away from me.

TRAFFICKER: Why?

MANAGER: Her eyes.

TRAFFICKER: They plugholes too? Or plug sockets?

MANAGER: They see more than they should see.

TRAFFICKER: Yours are no fucking postcards either. It's called
trauma; she got trauma – a symptom of civil war.

MANAGER: There's more to see under the earth than above it.

TRAFFICKER: Bastard boy, it's been a pleasure. Bedoon fuck.
(To the GIRL.) Come here.

GIRL: When are we leaving?

TRAFFICKER: I need you to meet my nephew; he studied in
America, he's very devout – don't you dare take off your hijab.

GIRL: What took him to America?

TRAFFICKER: Hypocrisy!

*TRAFFICKER ushers the GIRL into the CASHIER's cabin, then makes
his way hastily across the forecourt and behind the FATHER's cabin.
The MANAGER watches them.*

MANAGER: See it fall across the earth; a shadow, unfolding like a birth...
I'm waiting, wondering if you've come,
To seal this hole like an open mouth is closed by a thumb.
There won't be another chance,
And if there is, it's when the throne is broken and all the trees are stumps.

SCENE FIVE

KHAN: Yes, sir.

CASHIER: *(Seated, trying to catch a mosquito above his head.)*
You want your passport to transfer a large amount of money to your mother who is about to undergo major surgery, Khan, is that right?

KHAN: Yes, sir.

CASHIER: What kind of operation?

KHAN: Heart surgery, sir.

CASHIER: How much money, Khan?

KHAN: $500.

CASHIER: And this money will save her life, will it?

KHAN: It is in the hands of God, sir.

CASHIER: Passport request refused, Khan.

KHAN: But, sir.

CASHIER: Good morning, Khan. You're digging too hard for my liking. Dig less, dig much less and ask for your passport again in a week or two.

KHAN: But then Manager sir will beat me, sir.

CASHIER: Tell Bayu. He's got more brains than you.

KHAN: But, sir, my mother –

CASHIER: But sir, good morning, sir, best wishes to the Mama and goodbye Khan.

KHAN: Good morning, sir.

KHAN exits and returns to work on the forecourt.

GIRL: I was told to wait in here.

CASHIER: It's much cooler.

GIRL: Yes.

CASHIER: Pepsi, Seven-Up? Something stronger? We have everything.

GIRL: Nothing, thank you.

CASHIER: Joseph, water with ice, quickly.

GIRL: *(Removing her veil.)* At last.

CASHIER: That was fast! *(Holding up his phone to take a photograph.)*

GIRL: I never thought light could be so thick…or blood so thin…

CASHIER: Don't flinch; I won't share it.

GIRL: Two days in that truck: the stink of men's eyes. Damn you, God.

CASHIER: How about a cool shower? I've English towels.

GIRL: Water's fine.

(She takes a handful of ice cubes and puts her hand beneath her abbat, to lower them onto her chest.)

CASHIER: So, how do you like our station?

GIRL: Its charm is in its residents.

CASHIER: You know my Uncle, obviously. You've met my half-brother, the stateless Bedoon.

GIRL: Are you a Bedoon?

CASHIER: Do I look like a Bedoon?

GIRL: What does a Bedoon look like?

CASHIER: Shit. I, like my father, am a national of the first degree.

GIRL: How can your brother –

CASHIER: Half-brother, blighted by a whore of a mother. It's his own fault – forget him.

GIRL: Is there anyone else I should meet here?

CASHIER: A fistful of dogs.

GIRL: Dogs can be nobler than men.

Noon prayers from the minaret.

CASHIER: This is not my ambition.

GIRL: What is your ambition?

CASHIER: Neighbourly feeling.

GIRL: Ha.

CASHIER: Commerce and free trade. The unhindered movement of people, goods and trade: the only true pillars of neighbourly feeling.

GIRL: Smuggle petrol into a warzone, sell it to mercenaries to trade it for machetes to swing into the chests of children: commerce and free trade?

CASHIER: It's still phase one. Bloody, unpleasant but in movement.

GIRL: Towards?

CASHIER: Everything you see now, everything out there; the piles of dead earth, uncleared mines, prickly scrub and unmarked graves, the whole sad, sorry accumulation of piss-management, bearded zealots and rusty Empire are all just parcels of unused potential, awaiting transformation. Fast track to the future *(Turning the lights on the model town.)* This is the future. I'm their transformer.

GIRL: *(Pointing to a fountain in the model.)* What's this?

CASHIER: Bellagio Fountain, but bigger. This is the Eiffel Tower, but bigger. Big Ben –

GIRL: But bigger.

CASHIER: Exactly. Look, here's the Central Entertainment Zone; an air-conditioned pedestrian village that twists and turns like an ancient souk, with panoramic vistas studded into it that open onto Austrian foothills, Venetian lagoons, Norwegian lakes. Some real, some painted – I'm looking into holograms. Every retail space is either a massage parlour, or a drinking establishment. Pub, bar, tavern, izakaya you name it, you'll find it. Fine dining in this row, falafel and kebab shops in that one. The booths along this middle axis back onto the central atrium: a giant marble-clad dome the size of a football stadium that houses the biggest gambling arena in the world. Roulette tables, one-armed bandits, blackjack, girded from the mezzanine up by a seven-star hotel – helipad on the roof, pole dancing in the basement. It's called 'Firdous', you know, like paradise.

GIRL: Who's this for?

CASHIER: Soldiers on leave, mercenaries on downtime, Gulf sex addicts. Future prospects are astonishing, I've got Chinese money interested, we're talking thirty percent return on IBIDA by year six.

GIRL: This is your ambition?

CASHIER: It's why I came back.

GIRL: –

CASHIER: What do you think?

GIRL: It's an abomination.

CASHIER: No, no, you don't get it: this is society building.

GIRL: What kind of society?

CASHIER: A peaceful, sustainable one based on the pursuit of pleasure.

GIRL: Slavery and debauch leads to peace and prosperity?

CASHIER: Where's the slavery?

GIRL: You!

CASHIER: N'ha-ha. I have the vision. All I need is the start-up capital; then it's game over –

GIRL: Is this your ambition? This plastic Eldorado for dirty old men! Where were you educated? Let me guess, NYU, Colombia, MIT? And this is the sum total of your privilege: what use are you to your people? You're worse than an enemy: you are a traitor.

CASHIER: I never wore the Che Guevara t-shirt if that's –

GIRL: What their armies couldn't do to my people with bombs and bullets, they've done to your type with MBAs, free porn and drive-in meals. Do you know the difference between Bayat, Hijaz and Ajam, do you know the difference between scales used for love and war?

CASHIER: When was the last time a Sumerian made an app?

GIRL: They invented writing.

CASHIER: Wrong century.

GIRL: You've been gutted, razed, blasted, you are pap; all that's left of you is an olive-skinned shell. The Semite, the Akkadian, the Babylonian, the Nabataean, the Jew and the Arab all cower within you, all dead husks. You prancing, walking genocide –

CASHIER: Walking Genocide, what a great name for an arcade!

GIRL: Our house is on fire! The flames that consume us over that border, will reach your roofs soon.

CASHIER: Yeah, that's why we're going to sell you more petrol. *(Taking out a mobile phone.)* Classical, Gypsy, Lounge? What did you say your name was?

GIRL: Khadija.

CASHIER: Fancy. You're too young for a name like that. *(Plays music from his phone.)* Dance, Khadija, show me your body, or I'll film you being raped.

(Pause.)

GIRL: Pour me whiskey.

(He serves her. She drinks. She begins to dance slowly, with her eyes closed.)

GIRL: I hear there's a reward for illegal immigrants like me. How much am I worth?

CASHIER: Five.

GIRL: Dollars?

CASHIER: Local. $12,000.

GIRL: Do you like fast cars?

CASHIER: You buying or selling?

GIRL: Both.

CASHIER: Want to ride?

GIRL: What you got?

CASHIER: *(Withdrawing keys from a drawer.)* A dirty, white pickup.

GIRL: *(Suggestively.)* Mmmm.

CASHIER: Well?

GIRL: Sounds good to me.

CASHIER: Take off your bra.

(She laughs.)

CASHIER: I said take off your bra, show me your –

GIRL: *(Laughing uncontrollably.)* You're a virgin! Just like she was! But could she ever, ever love you?

CASHIER: A girl like you came through here a few months back, I took her to a party in the desert and she got liquor in her veins and started mouthing politics; so my friends took her behind the Mustang and –

GIRL: *(Taking out the knife.)* Silence your filthy mouth! *(He stops the music.)* Here, *(Removing a lapis and gold necklace.)* It was my Grandmother's. It's lapis and gold.

CASHIER: *(Taking the necklace.)* Do I look like a U.N. refugee official?

GIRL: You'll have more if you get me my papers.

CASHIER: Walking cash point. Does your husband know?

GIRL: Do you know how powerfully fate has turned upon me?

CASHIER: *(Mocking.)* More powerful than a horse turning on a battle plain!

GIRL: Virgin rich boy, pale as the moon: shall I be your courtesan?

CASHIER: Time makes dogs into men and courtesans of us all.

GIRL: Dizzy. More whiskey. Maybe you next? Fetch me ice.

CASHIER: Joseph!

GIRL: Not Joseph! Ice from your hands.

CASHIER: *(Opening the door to leave the cabin.)* What did you say your name was?

GIRL: Hurry.

The CASHIER exits the booth. She opens the drawer and removes the keys to the Pickup truck. JOSEPH, standing on the other side of the glass window, stares at her back. She turns around: they stare at one another. A figure climbs out of the manhole at the top of the petrol tanker and slides down the shell to the far side, unseen. The GIRL, still staring at JOSEPH, removes her bra and leaves it on the table, then exits. The light is speckled and hybrid, the sky is black with oil. The dust rises in bursts.

NOAH climbs out of the manhole at the top of the petrol tanker and slides down the shell to the far side, unseen.

SCENE SIX

(BAYU and KHAN, digging.)

[31]**BAYU:** তোর বেচারি মা ।

[32]**KHAN:** কেন?

[33]**BAYU:** তোর মতন একটা ছাগলের জন্ম দিলো। তোকে ছাগলের মতন দেখতে, কেউ বলেনি তোকে?

[34]**KHAN:** থাম, বায়ু ।

[35]**BAYU:** আল্লার কসম, তুই বড় মিষ্টি ছাগল – আয় তোকে নিয়ে মজা করি । বয়া !

[36]**KHAN:** ছাড় আমাকে! দেখ ।

---

[31]BAYU: Poor thing, your mother.

[32]KHAN: Why?

[33]BAYU: Giving birth to a goat like you. You look like a goat. Nobody told you?

[34]KHAN: Enough now, Bayu.

[35]BAYU: By Allah, you're a pretty goat, come here let me fuck you! Baaa!

[36]KHAN: Off me! Look!

Enter NOAH, bleeding, delirious.

NOAH: Give me water.

BAYU: No water.

NOAH: Water!

BAYU: No water, no laban, no carpets, no shade.

NOAH: Which dog was trying to seduce her?

KHAN: He's bleeding, Bayu.

NOAH: North, where is North?

BAYU: Who are you?

NOAH: A Prince who suffers misfortune.

BAYU: And I am a King! This pit is my Kingdom and this spade, my sceptre!

NOAH: Black-headed demons!

BAYU: Khan, clean my hands. Clean hands needed to receive royalty.

NOAH: A day's walk from here, a thousand men work across donums of palms that stretch farther along the river than bodies can float. Mullahs carve my name into the tiles of mosques and boys onto their chests with razors.

BAYU: The signs of doomsday are gathering fast, Khan.

KHAN: What signs?

NOAH: Which way North?

BAYU: When princes ask favours of beggars. Get the rope.

---

[37] KHAN: *(Hushed.)* Bayu, he sounds like a Prince.

NOAH: By these drops of blood that fall into your pit of filth I swear to make those who befriend me masters and those who defy me into slaves.

[37]**KHAN:** *(Hushed.)* বায়ু, রাজপুত্তুরের মতো লাগছে ।

[38]**BAYU:** বেআইনি ইমিগর্য্যান্ট – একে ১০ বছর খাটান যাবে। এর পেছনে যা । *(To NOAH.)* North is that way. Tell me about the North.

NOAH: In the North, a bomb has fallen from the giant's hand and made the great rivers flood their banks, the day is bruised and bloodstained; the night a mutilated sex.

[39]**KHAN:** কত দাম হবে রে এর, বায়ু ?

[40]**BAYU:** অনেক । আস্তে । *(To NOAH.)* Tell us more.

NOAH: The sun is dark, the urns have cracked, the skins have split; the sky is shattered, no rain can clean the rot –

(BAYU and KHAN lunge at NOAH. NOAH pulls out a Glock pistol from a leather chest holster beneath his shirt and places its muzzle firmly in BAYU's stomach.)

KHAN: Bayu!

BAYU: Sorry! Sorry!

NOAH: Where is the bullet?

BAYU: Sorry!

NOAH: Where is the bullet?

BAYU: In the gun.

---

[38]BAYU: Illegal immigrant. He's ten years' worth of hard labour. Move behind him.

[39]KHAN: How much is he worth, Bayu?

[40]BAYU: A lot, slowly.

NOAH: And when I pull the trigger, where is the bullet?
Where is the bullet?

BAYU: Here.

NOAH: Where?

BAYU: In my belly.

NOAH: Are you sure?

(NOAH pulls the trigger: the pistol is not loaded.)

BAYU: Ah!

(NOAH pushes BAYU to the ground and loads the pistol.)

NOAH: You are alive because I kept you alive.

BAYU: Yes.

NOAH: Why are you alive?

BAYU: Because you.

NOAH: Your life belongs to who? Who?

(NOAH puts the pistol into BAYU's mouth.)

BAYU: You.

NOAH: Don't forget it. *(To KHAN.)* Get the other guns.

KHAN: Where from?

NOAH: My sister needs two pillows under her neck, not one!
The fumes weakened her, her chest is not good!
When she wakes, tell me, only she can read these dreams.
Where's the bastard who taints her honour?

(NOAH collapses. BAYU and KHAN carry NOAH into their shack, watched by JOSEPH.)

ACT TWO

SCENE ONE

JOSEPH crosses the forecourt carrying box files into the FATHER's cabin.

MANAGER: It's no accident.

GIRL: I'm going to the truck.

MANAGER: The meter, the digging, then you.

GIRL: Let me pass.

MANAGER: I know why you're here.

GIRL: Don't touch me!

MANAGER: I – sorry – I'm blind. Tell me what you see.

GIRL: Nothing worth seeing.

MANAGER: Describe what you see, then go.

GIRL: Three shacks and a tree.

MANAGER: And?

GIRL: No women anywhere.

MANAGER: And?

GIRL: A prison with no walls, starvation without hunger, a sun with no mercy; even the air begs oxygen.

MANAGER: More.

GIRL: There's nothing more.

MANAGER: I can't write. I mean, read some: *(Pointing to a sign and reading with rigidity.)* EXIT; but write, no, not write. See things; name them. Keep more names for things than there are things because moisture in the soil and the sun's lurching shift them. Watch, name, remember, rename. But then you: your back towards me, your legs long as palms, your eyes green as the sea, never seen anything like you before and now all the names I had for things crumble like dry earth. The world's filling with blanks, there's more light in my skull than the sky is round and it's blinding. Never wanted to write before, never needed to. Time could approach and time could pass and it wouldn't matter. Now I want to seize time, stop it, hold it still where I can...

GIRL: What?

MANAGER: You are a new alphabet. Teach me you.

GIRL: Teach you me to what?

MANAGER: Write.

GIRL: To mark me down as chattel, tattoo my ankles, label my digits?

MANAGER: To write the world again.

GIRL: *(With lightness.)* Had we but world enough and time[41]

MANAGER: Mock. I spoke.

GIRL: Name me then the letters of my alphabet.

MANAGER: Don't know them.

GIRL: You spoke: now name one.

MANAGER: A head of corn ripening.

GIRL: Another.

MANAGER: A river fish turning.

GIRL: Then?

MANAGER: A wet lip drying.

---

[41] A.Marvell, *To His Coy Mistress*

GIRL: Then?

MANAGER: A throat filling with song.

GIRL: Name the last letter.

MANAGER: I don't know it – you won't leave.

GIRL: Stop me!

MANAGER: I'll help you, be your guide.

GIRL: Illiterate, babbling, blind man guide!

MANAGER: I took an advance – you gave it!

GIRL: In panic.

MANAGER: A gage, a down payment!

GIRL: I'm out of my world, into another darker, nether world but I'm not lining up to join the ranks of the dispossessed. I've a people that need me, a country on the slaughter rack, seized in the pains of a terrible becoming. Out of this bloodshed, out of this suffering a child is being born; a child that if left motherless will be defaced by monsters and grow into a ghoul so callused and pitiless that for centuries no books, no grants, no armies will undo the horror. I've pledged my life to this unborn child and vowed to teach it all I know and all I love and all I wish for. That is my alphabet. The rest is flesh and rutting in the dust. Keep the down payment, I don't need you.

The GIRL moves forcefully towards the truck. The MANAGER stays on the forecourt, perfectly still. The dust swirls in ribbons around him, he calls the Mid-Afternoon prayers. The CASHIER returns to his cabin.

CASHIER: Where's she gone?

JOSEPH: To hunt.

CASHIER: Cunts and black skies!

JOSEPH: The wind is rising.

CASHIER: Feel it in my throat.

JOSEPH: Put this towel under the door.

CASHIER: Wet it first.

JOSEPH: It is. *(Lays the towel along the foot of the door frame.)* Baba.

CASHIER: What?

JOSEPH: The meter.

CASHIER: What about it?

JOSEPH: I know where it is.

> *(Pause. The GIRL, standing by the truck, pierces the tires of the Tanker with the knife.)*

CASHIER: Who else knows?

JOSEPH: Nobody.

CASHIER: Where is it?

JOSEPH: It's there.

CASHIER: Where?

JOSEPH: Where I buried it still.

CASHIER: Where exactly?

JOSEPH: *(JOSEPH's eyes well with tears.)* It's a terrible thing.

CASHIER: Where's the meter?

JOSEPH: God knows it.

CASHIER: Oh, traitor.

JOSEPH: I've come to you, baba.

CASHIER: Oh, little ball of filth.

JOSEPH: I keep the secrets Baba: all inside me.

CASHIER: I don't like inflicting violence, Joseph.

JOSEPH: This mouth does not speak.

CASHIER: I'm a coward by nature, a sadist by inclination.

JOSEPH: This mouth is tired.

CASHIER: I can see violence, watch it with relish –

JOSEPH: This mouth is heavy.

CASHIER: … Through violence I perceive a truer blueprint of the world than is contained in a thousand acts of pity.

JOSEPH: But my chest is thin and tight with fear.

CASHIER: Tell me what you know.

JOSEPH: Because God knows.

CASHIER: Or I'll take your fingers –

JOSEPH: He will send for Joseph.

CASHIER: And plant their tips –

JOSEPH: Joseph cannot but go to God.

CASHIER: In the hinges of this door.

JOSEPH: You must not know, do not ask.

CASHIER: Where's that cattle prod I ordered off Amazon?

JOSEPH: She the girl, the girl with no veil, with no bra, with no necklace and a hundred names, she –

CASHIER: Joseph, you're foaming at the mouth!

JOSEPH: She comes to avenge her dead!

CASHIER: What dead? Don't breathe on me! Away, shoo!

JOSEPH: The last time the skies were dark they came in swarms and droves; you weren't born, there were no fences then. All carrying what their frames could hold, with string and wire and death-hollowed faces, they set up rough camp against the northern ridge. Rich men pulled gold teeth from their own mouths to exchange, caked in blood, for warm milk and poor men dragged stiff-legged daughters across the sand for bags of dried shrimp. Your father bought a girl. She had emerald eyes and when she walked onto the forecourt he placed a necklace of lapis and gold on her neck and slaughtered a fold of sheep for her kin by the ridge. Charity, he said, human feeling, he said, leads us away from our intentions. He took her to his bed, for many nights he took her. Once, he washed this girl's feet with sweet water under your mother's eyes. At that time Mama was pregnant with you and she made him swear on the life of the unborn child never to marry the girl and to force this pledge she took a knife to her swollen stomach and he swore it. On the days Baba went to the city, your mother had the girl chase snakes from the well barefoot, 'Dirt from my fingernails!' and she beat her, 'Sleep with the stray dogs,' and she beat her, 'I want to see your vagina swell with the poison of scorpions!'. When the darkness peeled from the skies and the sun came again, the girl was pregnant and a terrible silence filled the station. On the day of pain, no doctor was called and no bed was laid, under the tree she squatted, her teeth gnawing on a branch, her cries so terrible we filled our ears with wax –

(The FATHER rings the bell.)

CASHIER: Shut up! Shut up!

JOSEPH: No one must ever know.

CASHIER: See what my father wants. Put him straight back to sleep.

(JOSEPH exits. The CASHIER uncovers the model city and destroys it with his hands. The FATHER emerges from his cabin and the CASHIER sees him.)

CASHIER: Shit!

SCENE TWO

(The FATHER walks slowly and deliberately towards the pumps and the truck. The digging stops, a dense silence fills the station. Only the FATHER appears to move, whilst the others stand in a still apprehension.)

FATHER: Son!

CASHIER: *(Over the tannoy.)* Yes, Baba. *(The tannoy does not function. The CASHIER shouts the words from inside the cabin.)*

FATHER: In Hell, will your brother burn alone or will you burn first? *(To himself.)* No compassion in those dugs, no charity in those loins. *(To CASHIER.)* Bring your brother a chilled glass of water. Carry mercy in your hands: do not spill a drop. I will hear the drop. The sound of it will explode in my heart and I will hate you. *(To the MANAGER.)* Son, don't move, water will come to you.

(The TRAFFICKER emerges from the FATHER's cabin.)

FATHER: When she comes, send her to me. Grief, like a garment, covers the horizon. The liar is here. It will come to pass.

(The FATHER regains the inside of his cabin, the door closes behind him. The TRAFFICKER remains on the veranda, lights a cigarette. A low sibilance fills the air. The CASHIER moves out of his booth, carrying a glass of water across the forecourt, with two hands. The sun is low on the horizon.)

SCENE THREE

On the forecourt.

TRAFFICKER: I left my wife with you, nephew, where is she?

CASHIER: Do I look like a UN refugee official?

TRAFFICKER: What happened? What did she show you?

CASHIER: Take your bitch, take your truck and fuck off. It's official: today is a bad day for smuggling.

TRAFFICKER: No, I've been talking to your father about it.

CASHIER: About what?

TRAFFICKER: My dilemma.

CASHIER: What fucking dilemma?

TRAFFICKER: He's very lucid when it comes to affairs of the heart. Where did she go?

CASHIER: I took her up the arse and she fled.

TRAFFICKER: Liar.

CASHIER: She wouldn't have it any other way. Consolation, isn't it? Flower intact etcetera.

TRAFFICKER: I'd pickle my cock in a jerry can if you could deflower a piece of frozen poultry. Where is she? Hafsa!

CASHIER: One drop of this water, a solitary drop and that's my whole inheritance down the guzzler. He'll strike me out with a shaking, blue-veined hand. Decimation: a life of penury and hard labour for which I am in no way prepared. Then I'll come for you with a drone. Get your truck off this station.

TRAFFICKER: My tires are slashed.

CASHIER: What?

TRAFFICKER: Joseph!

CASHIER: Oh, mother.

TRAFFICKER: *(To BAYU.)* Was this you, dirty Bangla?

BAYU: Not me Baba, not me.

TRAFFICKER: Joseph, son of a whore, come here!

JOSEPH approaches the TRAFFICKER.

JOSEPH: Take her away.

TRAFFICKER: Who slashed my tires?

JOSEPH: Take her away!

TRAFFICKER: Three fucking tires!

JOSEPH: She has no place here.

TRAFFICKER: Damn right, Jo-Jo, call this a seven-star hotel?

JOSEPH: Hair. Claws.

TRAFFICKER: Bring down the luggage, Maysab, call my driver, chop-chop, we're checking out of this establishment this instant!

JOSEPH: In the Upper Nile where waters seep from the blood red earth –

TRAFFICKER: 315 over 85 Michelin tires.

JOSEPH: When the rains hoe the skull-capped earth –

TRAFFICKER: Not Korean, not Chinese, Michelin!

JOSEPH: A serpent writhes out of the reeds and takes the body of a woman!

TRAFFICKER: Yankee Generals whistled at these tires!

JOSEPH: Snake woman, oiled in multiple, aqueous greens, her sex so potent men bolt from sleep and reach for daggers. Across the village she rides her haunches and they, with sleep filled eyes; fathers, brothers, sons no more, those village men in twos, fours; in sevens and nines, all mud and gore, their knives churning like a gyre – frenzy now – lurching limbs and dicing flesh and she, shimmying slow, behind her serpent sex plaits the earth with blood like a bridal gown –

TRAFFICKER: Joseph, I don't see any rivers, Joseph: I see three slashed tires.

JOSEPH: Because there's a dagger in your fist.

> (*TRAFFICKER punches JOSEPH in the stomach JOSEPH collapses, winded.*)

TRAFFICKER: Khan bay!

KHAN: Khalloo sab!

TRAFFICKER: I've a letter from home for you. Remind me later. Change these fucking tires.

KHAN: Yes, sir.

> *(The CASHIER continues his trajectory, transporting the glass of water across the forecourt. Ribbons of dust surround him and his hands begin to tremble. Over the tannoy we hear a woman's voice, close, intimate but distorted, on the edge of audibility. The CASHIER is hallucinating. The voice is his MOTHER's.)*

MOTHER: *(Voice only.)* Why are your nails so dirty and your mouth so dry, your shoes so tattered your eyes so yellow, your hair so long and your back so bent? Look at your mother when she speaks to you!

CASHIER: I –

MOTHER: Are you Arab? Or a freak these loins have borne?

CASHIER: Mother, I –

MOTHER: Stay where you are, whelp, you're not free to forego what I earned for you with blood: this is your second birth: the pain of it is on you! There is no justice, there is none, don't wait for it to come, if it does the whore child will eat your liver. He knows his roots: you've forgotten yours. Drop the glass! Smash it! Cut down that tree, cut down all the trees, burn all the branches, split every root, wet your lips in his blood.

> *The CASHIER drops the glass of water, the sun slips below the horizon, darkness gathers like flies onto a peeled hide.*

> *Maghrib – sunset – prayers are sounded from the minaret. The halogen floodlights begin to warm up and emit aqueous light.*

SCENE FOUR

Inside the CASHIER's booth.

TRAFFICKER: Made you tea. Where've you been?

GIRL: In the desert.

TRAFFICKER: Who with?

GIRL: My ancestors.

(He laughs. She laughs.)

TRAFFICKER: About family…

GIRL: What about it?

TRAFFICKER: I worry about your brother.

GIRL: Why?

TRAFFICKER: He's your only surviving relative. Shouldn't have left him back there; the boy's mixed up, in with the wrong people, junked on Captagon, he'll get himself killed. I could go back for him.

GIRL: There's a kind of compassion that comes off the back of heat. Out there, under the sun, it's so hot that violence is superfluous. But here in this little cabin, it's so cold and devoid of dust…that somehow; the evil in man finds leisure to bloom.

TRAFFICKER: *(Turns off the air conditioning.)* There. Just the sound of compassion.

GIRL: Don't worry about my brother.

TRAFFICKER: I'd do anything for you.

GIRL: When are we leaving?

TRAFFICKER: What's the rush?

GIRL: Take me to the city – that was our deal.

TRAFFICKER: Deals develop in international affairs. Don't you like it here?

GIRL: I need to get to a hospital.

TRAFFICKER: Why? What's wrong?

GIRL: I've a female concern.

TRAFFICKER: What kind?

GIRL: Doesn't matter.

TRAFFICKER: I'm an expert in female concerns. Used to trade with the maternity nurses: painkillers for Russian cigarettes –

GIRL: It's nothing: I just need a hospital.

TRAFFICKER: Nothing? Nothing needs no hospital, baby.

GIRL: Fuck you!

TRAFFICKER: Is that any way to speak to your betrothed? You are my wife, Hafsa!

GIRL: I'm nobody's wife, pig.

TRAFFICKER: I've a marriage certificate. By God and his Prophet I've got one. Apostilled by legal experts at the border; it stands on both sides.

GIRL: Do you know what happened to me while you sat smoking with the legal experts?

TRAFFICKER: You were in the truck.

GIRL: Yes: in the truck!

TRAFFICKER: What?

GIRL: You think a woman is a piece of porcelain –

TRAFFICKER: What happened to you?

GIRL: …wrapped in paper?

TRAFFICKER: Was it that filthy tribesman?

GIRL: She was young and very shy.

TRAFFICKER: The new border manager – Piss! – was it him?

GIRL: Pretty and full of promise.

TRAFFICKER: Is that why he whistled at me?

GIRL: She is no longer who she was.

TRAFFICKER: Hafsa!

GIRL: Who's she?

TRAFFICKER: Speak properly!

GIRL: No one did anything to me because I'm no longer one woman: I am many! Take my name, write it into contracts, take my body and abuse it: neither ink nor flesh can trace nor bind me. I'm charging through the gates of hell; at each gate violence onto this body, here, then here, then here, but I won't be reduced. *(She rips the contract. He falls to her feet.)*

TRAFFICKER: A thing has opened inside me.

GIRL: Like a cluster bomb, I'll multiply –

TRAFFICKER: It splits me in two.

GIRL: … Each detonation a flower –

TRAFFICKER: My entrails under your feet. I want to taste the honeycomb.

GIRL: … Each flower a new name!

TRAFFICKER: Give me my rights.

GIRL: What is this? *(To herself.)* Do not ask.

TRAFFICKER: Legal, god-honoured rights!

> *TRAFFICKER seizes the GIRL and tears at her clothes with both hands. He attempts to rape her.*

TRAFFICKER: Sharia rights!

GIRL: WHAT IS THIS?

TRAFFCIKER: Sharia rights!

GIRL: DO NOT ASK!

Enter MANAGER and bites TRAFFICKER viciously on the face. TRAFFICKER screams and falls to the ground. MANAGER and GIRL move onto the forecourt.

SCENE FIVE

MANAGER and GIRL, moving across the platform in haste.

GIRL: My brother's inside this truck.

MANAGER: Down payment just doubled.

(She kisses him and bites his lip viciously.)

MANAGER: You've drawn blood!

GIRL: The earth is thirsty.

MANAGER: *(Sees a trail of blood on the tarmac.)* Blood trails you like a gown.

GIRL: *(Calling.)* Noah!

MANAGER: Don't shout.

GIRL: Noah!

(The electricity cuts out and the Station falls into darkness.)

MANAGER: Space.

GIRL: Where is he?

MANAGER: Space.

GIRL: Take me to him.

(The tree rustles.)

MANAGER: Listen.

GIRL: Please, I beg you, he's all I have left –

MANAGER: She's speaking.

GIRL: Noah!

MANAGER: *(Calling to the tree.)* I'm here.

(MANAGER moves beyond the forecourt perimeter towards the tree. The GIRL stands alone on the forecourt. Surging from the semi darkness, JOSEPH places his hand over her mouth and whispers.)

JOSEPH: I have your brother. It's been arranged. Meet me at the pickup truck in twenty minutes. Lie down in the back, cover yourself with the blanket; I'll take you to the city. Come back and I'll kill you both, understand? Give me the key.

(She gives JOSEPH the key, he withdraws.)

MANAGER: *(At the perimeter.)* She knows it's you.

GIRL: Who?

MANAGER: Come.

GIRL: Where?

MANAGER: To meet her.

(She moves beyond the perimeter of the forecourt, towards the Cidra tree.)

SCENE SIX

BAYU and KHAN, lit by candles, dressing up as princes, listening to Indian pop. NOAH sleeping by a wall decorated with porn.

[42]**KHAN:** এতো মহিলা – চাকরাদি। আই ।

---

[42] KHAN: This is a woman, this is Chankra-Di! Aie!

[43]**BAYU:** কলকাতার বেড়াল। কলকাতার মেনি বেড়াল । দাড়া, রাজপুত্তুর। রাজপুত্তুরের জন্য় কাজল ।

[44]**KHAN:** আরো , আরো লাগা

[45]**BAYU:** খুব সাধারণ জিনিস নিয়ে কথা বলবি – শুধু থাকা-খাওয়ার ব্যবস্থার কথা বলবি।

[46]**KHAN:** খাবার রেস্তেরা তো জানিনা ।

[47]**BAYU:** যে কোনো নাম বলে তার পরে "মহল" বা "প্য়ালেস" জুড়ে দিবি । হাত ঝাকিয়ে নে , আধবোজা চোখ – এইতো বড়লোক লাগছে। এবার গলাটা –

(NOAH groans.)

[48]**KHAN:** এ তো জেগে উঠছে, আর আমি এখনো রাজপুত্র হইনি!

(BAYU turns off the music.)

NOAH: Bring me –

[49]**BAYU:** ওকে দেখ তুই

[50]**KHAN:** আমার মাথা খেল ।

---

[43]BAYU: Calcutta Cat, Calcutta Pussy Cat – wait Prince, kohl for the Prince!

[44]KHAN: More, more! Give me some rings!

[45]BAYU: Talk as generally as you can, be specific only about restaurants and travel arrangements,

[46]KHAN: I don't know any restaurants.

[47]BAYU: Take any name and say Palace after it, or Mahal. Fingers loose, move your hands from the wrist, eyes half shut: you're beginning to look wealthy. Now the voice –

[48]KHAN: He's waking up and I'm not yet a Prince!

[49]BAYU: Watch him!

[50]KHAN: Wrecking my pussy wall!

NOAH: Bring me –

[51]KHAN: রাজকুমারীকে চটাচ্ছ ।

[52]BAYU: ওদেরকে দূর কর, শালা বাঁদর ।

NOAH: *(Pulls a crumpled green bandana out of his pocket.)* Bring me the oppressed and I will liberate them!

(JOSEPH observes them, unseen.)

SCENE SEVEN

(MANAGER kneeling by the Cidra tree, laying rice, dates, pomegranate as at a shrine.)

MANAGER: I hear my mother's voice under this tree.

GIRL: How long dead?

MANAGER: Not dead: sent away. She lives. Gave birth to me unmarried, then forced to leave. My brother's mother is white. Women on women are harder than stone on flesh.

GIRL: Have you ever –

MANAGER: No. Blanks don't cross borders.

GIRL: Blanks?

MANAGER: I'm a Bedoon!
Place of birth? Blank.
Occupation? Blank.
Sex? Blank.
Mother's name? Blank.
Nationality? Blank.
Born here, bred here, blank.

---

[51]KHAN: Upsetting the Princesses.

[52]BAYU: Get rid of them, spunk monkey!

GIRL: I crossed the border and became stateless.

MANAGER: Yours is a temporary affliction.

GIRL: And your pain is vast as a lake. Drink from it and let it poison you.

MANAGER: I'm not bitter.

GIRL: You've no right to bitterness, beggar!

MANAGER: I'm no beggar.

GIRL: You are what your father has made you: a beggar.

MANAGER: He gave me his love; his love is my universe.

GIRL: *(Impersonating a patriarchal mullah.)* 'Know that you are my slave.' Say: Allah u Akbar!

MANAGER: Will you question God's will?

GIRL: I saw my father murdered and my mother die silent like a bird that's been stoned, and you ask if I'll question God's will? I will question it! My being is a question mark! And you, hypocrite, don't you question?

MANAGER: Never.

GIRL: Then why do you dig?

MANAGER: It's God's will.

GIRL: Why?

MANAGER: To find the meter.

GIRL: Why?

MANAGER: To give the past its voice!

GIRL: What past? What voice?

MANAGER: The past is mute, its injustice unspoken.

GIRL: Then fate has done you wrong and you question it! You dig to resist it, you dig to fight it, you work to undo it!

MANAGER: Yes, I dig to undo what has been wrongly done and give the mute past tongue.

GIRL: Tongue to speak what?

MANAGER: That what I've endured has not been in vain, that murder is not the only option.

(Pause. She stands looking at the solemn red disc of a low, full moon.)

GIRL: Scorpio moon over the Petrol Station: the dead charge towards us and we to Pluto headlong tack. I loathe shrines.

Undress me.
Undress me now!
My body is taller than the minaret.
Worship this body.

(He undresses her. She is naked. He is kneeled before her in amazement.)

You will never find the meter: the meter is inside you.

The silhouette of the minaret shrinks as the GIRL's body grows larger than life.

The TRAFFICKER approaches sheepishly and steals a flash photograph of the GIRL.

The flash light explodes like a cancer cell.

ACT THREE

SCENE ONE

Ballad in the American style of Johnny Cash, performed by CASHIER and, played on guitar by TRAFFICKER.

During the song the ensemble of actors dance, as at a ball.

CASHIER: I dream of you in my mind's eye,
Found a place for us to love,
Limpid as a lullaby
Show you the road; ride my cloud;
Heading where wild roses pound
And fairies patter with no sound:
Here our love can go to ground,
Yeah, here our love can go to ground.

Take this vein green as the sea
Firm as twine tied to a tree
Lay it on your pearly teeth
Cleave the tissue, watch it spurt,
Rain from heaven cleans the dirt
Hot as bitumen, sheer as rye,
Burning, burning my bad eye

Here's how the story goes,
Watch how my derrick blows:
Ring all the poor and wrong of race
Line'em up and giv'em Grace
Strip'em bare, sweet creatures fair,
Mount'em up, onto the truck,

Casings melt like leaves of lettuce
Metal shreds like finest dresses
A horn blows the tmypani
A peeling, feral melody
Hair loose to the wind!

Bodies melt like Vaseline
Pumping up the Ketamine
Babies drop like balls of dew
Into a bowl of azure hue
Here it goes, hear it roar
Keep it real, keep it raw
As God's my witness the sky was blue…

> *TRAFFICKER interrupts playing the guitar to move amongst the waltzing bodies. He delivers the monologue in frenzy of panic and paranoia. The CASHIER continues to hum the melody of the Ballad.*

TRAFFICKER: The Bedoon fuck's on the rampage. He moves without a sound. He's like that. Fast as scorpion. Even as a boy. Silent as the wind. Learnt subterfuge from his mother. The gypsy whore – No! She was a Jewess! No, no she was Shia! No, no, no: she was a Shia-Gypsy-Jewess. He could be anywhere: under the window, behind the wall. His mouth was wide open; two rows of teeth. His eyes were bloodshot, his neck was puffed, he had the force of ten men in him. Aaagh!

CASHIER: Splendour, splendour
Blazing fender,
Earth to mine,
deep pit of lime.

Never again I'll hear you cry:
I'm opening up my lullaby.
'Cos I dream of you
In my mind's eye…
Where our love goes to ground.

> *The dancing has ended, the ensemble disperses.*

> *In the wake of the dance, the platform is littered with guns. The TRAFFICKER is showing the CASHIER the photo of the GIRL.*

TRAFFICKER: He'll come for you next. It's you he wants dead. He wants this station.

CASHIER: He can't have it.

TRAFFICKER: His birth right.

CASHIER: He hasn't a birth certificate, what birth right?

TRAFFICKER: He's not afraid any more.

CASHIER: It's her!

TRAFFICKER: Forget her.

CASHIER: Gets butt naked for the man: gone and made him fearless.

TRAFFICKER: Knew she was trouble.

CASHIER: Let him out of his pen, given him ideas above his station.

TRAFFICKER: Jezebel!

CASHIER: Bet he's fucking her now.

TRAFFICKER: No.

CASHIER: Down in the ditch.

TRAFFICKER: Open the door.

CASHIER: She wants him.

TRAFFICKER: Son of a Shia, Gypsy, Jewess!

CASHIER: Bang, bang, bang!

TRAFFICKER: Filthy bastard Bedoon!

CASHIER: Yes, she says!

TRAFFICKER: Bites my face, fucks my wife!

CASHIER: More, she says!

TRAFFICKER: I'll pull his intestines out of his throat –

CASHIER: Brave Abu Ghraib!

TRAFFICKER: I'll tie his legs to the truck!

CASHIER: Yes!

TRAFFICKER: And draw him over the tarmac 'til his bones sing!

CASHIER: There's a man in you, cuckold!

TRAFFICKER: I'll feed him his own testicles!

CASHIER: Hang him from the Cidra tree!

TRAFFICKER: Bring me a rope, put the dagger in my fist –

CASHIER: It's a penknife.

TRAFFICKER: Does it puncture flesh?

CASHIER: At a push.

TRAFFICKER: Just give it to me!

(JOSEPH stands at the window.)

CASHIER / TRAFFICKER: *(In fright.)* Haa!

CASHIER: There's blood on his hands.

TRAFFICKER: Don't open the door.

CASHIER: He's writing in blood.

TRAFFICKER: What language?

CASHIER: English.

TRAFFICKER: What's he saying?

CASHIER: *(Reading.)* All…

TRAFFICKER: All what?

CASHIER: Done…

TRAFFICKER: Done what?

CASHIER: NOW …

TRAFFICKER: Where's he going? Joseph! Come back! Joseph! What the fuck does that mean?

CASHIER: Guns. There are guns.

TRAFFICKER: Where?

CASHIER: All over the forecourt.

TRAFFICKER: I can't see them.

CASHIER: Guns everywhere.

TRAFFICKER: Move.

CASHIER: It's a trap.

TRAFFICKER: I want them.

CASHIER: I'll watch you.

TRAFFICKER: Come with me you bastard.

CASHIER: If I ever declare independence from the state and create my own country, by God I'll make you Minister of Culture.

TRAFFICKER: Agriculture, Horticulture, anything but Culture!

CASHIER: Gather the flowers, gather the fruit, bring them here and I'll load them.

TRAFFICKER: Don't lock me out –

CASHIER: This is progress you pig!

TRAFFICKER: … Or I'll shoot you.

CASHIER: *(Over the tannoy.)* Global village ends here. History moves forward tonight; cull the faulty, behead the decrepit, show mercy to nothing but the pure of blood. No longer will the rightful owners of this Station live in fear on their own doorsteps: mongrels beware, half-blood scum and immigrants, death comes your way! Nothing not even poverty nothing swells the human gut with hatred like seasons of forced tolerance. Courage, Uncle, your blood is my blood and our guts are full of shit: go to harvest, the future is ours.

SCENE TWO

The tree rustles in the wind. Music.

MANAGER: Aisha, mama.

GIRL: What?

MANAGER: She's asking your name. My mother.

GIRL: How are you, my Aunt? You're the most beautiful thing I've seen since I left my home. Your son is a man he is kind, his heart is good, my Mother.

(The wind rises.)

Aisha died, mother, we will weep for her…
Hafsa? Hafsa was raped, mother, we will console her…
Khadija? Khadija blind wandered into the desert, we will mourn her…
Zeyneb? Yes, I am Zeyneb…
Maria[53]? She'll come later, at dawn perhaps, if ever that comes…

MANAGER: *(Weeping.)* I don't want it anymore.

GIRL: No.

MANAGER: I cannot have it anymore.

GIRL: No.

MANAGER: I cannot be this man anymore.

GIRL: Dig with me.

MANAGER: No.

GIRL: Dig here!

MANAGER: No more.

---

[53] Names of the wives of the Prophet Muhammed

GIRL: Your mother speaks to me.

MANAGER: What does she say?

GIRL: She says here, here is what you are looking for!

(He digs with his hands. The digging continues throughout the following scene. Out of the ground, the MANAGER unearths the long-decomposed remains of his dead mother.)

SCENE THREE

BAYU: We preferred, Prince Noah, to have our opening discussions in this humble desert retreat.

KHAN: Please accept this Rolex.

BAYU: Another gift, Khan: a car!

KHAN: Mercedes, BM or Cadillac?

BAYU: All three!!

NOAH: Your generosity overwhelms me, but I cannot accept gifts made by infidel nations.

KHAN: All fake, hajji, locally made fakes –

BAYU: Enough, Khan! We respect our guest's integrity and learn from it.

NOAH: I'm sorry my wounds do not permit me to speak more –

BAYU: You are a fighter; your wounds are marks of honour.

KHAN: And how are all the brothers?

NOAH: Thanks be to God.

KHAN: A thousand thanks to God: Mama survived the flood, too!

NOAH: Flood?

KHAN: Three chickens in a cage on her head she carried up the hill to Auntie's house, dickie heart and all.

BAYU: *(To NOAH.)* I apologise, my cousin hallucinates. He fancies his mother, my Aunt – who suffers nothing weightier than the burden of silks and precious stones on her, admittedly, obese body – imagines her a peasant, mugging through the Bay of Tigers – the very curse of rule.

NOAH: Nobility is cursed in ignoble times.

BAYU: *(To KHAN.)* More presents, Khan!

(KHAN exits.)

NOAH: Prince… Our struggle against the infidels has proved its moral supremacy; victory is just a matter of time.

BAYU: The divine promise will unfold.

NOAH: Fighting God's enemy is our duty, we accept it, but without the support of our brothers in the faith, our fighting is in vain. We need cash, weapons, food.

(KHAN re-enters carrying a wheel rim.)

BAYU: *(To KHAN.)* Get out!

KHAN: It's a hot rim, man!

BAYU: Out! *(To NOAH.)* Pray for him.

NOAH: Madness will swallow the Earth.

BAYU: With Holy War we sympathise, but your war is distant and our needs are pressing: it is time to bring war closer to home. Do you read me?

NOAH: Are you speaking for yourself, Prince, or on behalf of the state?

BAYU: And where do Princes end and States begin?

NOAH: What branch of the ruling family are you from?

BAYU: The deepest root.

NOAH: Honoured, but which branch is it?

BAYU: My tribesmen are everywhere and everywhere put out. My tribesmen are hungry for change, not shy of blood, see wealth in the hands of the few and feel the might of the many.

NOAH: Who are your tribesmen?

BAYU: The pill bearers, the dirt carriers, the cement throwers, the garbage cleaners, the eyes gleaming in the pipes, the bodies in the burning tires, the sutures in the wound. Indians, Pakistanis, Nepalese, Koreans, Thais, the dark and yellow skinned, the vengeful sperm of southern wolves that crept up the womb of the Gulf and mouth its ovaries. We the black armies of the black gold – will you lead us?

NOAH: You imitate your masters well.

BAYU: Because I hate them well.

NOAH: Where are we?

KHAN: Firdous Palace! Top notch, Paradise Mahal!

BAYU: Where are your guns?

NOAH: There was a woman travelling with me. Bring her to me and I'll fight with you.

BAYU: This is no time for women; the immigrants will revolt and you will lead them – where are your guns?

Enter TRAFFICKER carrying a gun.

KHAN: Khalloo-sab, not allowed in.

TRAFFICKER: *(To KHAN.)* Here's your letter. Your mother's dead. *(TRAFFICKER throws the letter to the floor.)*

KHAN: No, no, no, no. *(KHAN exits with the letter.)*

NOAH: Who are you?

TRAFFICKER: Your servant.

NOAH: Bone peddler?

TRAFFICKER: Rotten skiff skipper himself.

NOAH: Are we arrived in Kufa?

TRAFFICKER: This decadent land thirsts for the rule of righteous men.

NOAH: I've no enemies in this land.

TRAFFICKER: Is he who lets down your sister's hair, unclothes her body, stains your family honour no enemy?

BAYU: He's a liar!

(The TRAFFICKER turns the gun towards BAYU.)

BAYU: Shoot me!

TRAFFICKER: *(He shows NOAH the photograph of the GIRL on his phone.)* You know this chick?

Simultaneously on the platform, the MANAGER continues to dig frantically with his hands.

JOSEPH: *(Thrashing on the door of the FATHER's cabin.)* She's here! She's come! Wake up, wake up, wake up!

NOAH: Where is she?

(NOAH pulls aside the curtain of the cabin and reveals the silhouette of the MANAGER carrying the remains of an unearthed corpse across the forecourt.)

TRAFFICKER: Fuck.

JOSEPH: Not deep, no time, not deep enough. Her flesh asked so little dignity of sand. Lord! The watchman of this house trembles. Go, little man-soul, die.

NOAH: Who did this to her?

TRAFFICKER: *(Pointing to the MANAGER.)* An enemy of God and all good men. Take the gun, kill him.

The TRAFFICKER holds the gun out to NOAH. NOAH moves beyond the walls of the shack onto the platform, as if in a dilating moment of suspended time; the dialogue has the quality of dreams.

NOAH: Tell me you are not dead.

GIRL: Let me kiss you.

NOAH: Again. Again.

GIRL: You're bleeding.

NOAH: You're naked.

GIRL: It happened once before.

NOAH: When?

GIRL: I was seven you five; you down to your pants and me all prim in my smock frock. We played by the river and you fell, cut your head on a rock, went all blue trembling with cold and I took off my clothes to warm you. We walked back to the house you bleeding onto the smock, me shining naked.

NOAH: And you got punished.

GIRL: The frock was ruined! Came all the way from England!

NOAH: Where are we?

GIRL: Where the river spat us. Come, I'll heal your wounds; I'll make us a new home.

NOAH: No more homes.

GIRL: Don't fight with me.

NOAH: The bricks are too wet, the blood too fast.

GIRL: Don't need bricks.

NOAH: God will provide.

GIRL: Don't want God.

NOAH: Pills?

GIRL: All gone.

NOAH: Dogs are pouring out of the red hole.

GIRL: Shh…

NOAH: All teeth and hunger.

GIRL: Shh…

NOAH: They want to rip my flesh.

GIRL: Come with me.

NOAH: Why are you naked?

GIRL: Don't know.

NOAH: Where's your shame.

GIRL: What's that?

Slaps her.

GIRL: Birth.

NOAH: Saying?!

GIRL: Noah, look at me!

NOAH: You've turned, I see it in your eyes. You've turned against me!

GIRL: Put down your gun.

NOAH: Will you sacrifice me? Sacrifice your own brother!

GIRL: Stay with me.

NOAH: Tonight I die, sister. Don't shred your cheek in mourning; don't rip your clothes in grief!

GIRL: Shall I sing you to sleep?

NOAH moves back to the shack, the moment of suspended time retracts.

NOAH: I was a student of theology. But the pain of living overwhelmed my mind.

NOAH takes the gun from the TRAFFICKER. NOAH points the gun at the TRAFFICKER, then turns and points the gun at BAYU.

BAYU: *(To NOAH.)* Traitor!

NOAH: I no longer seek mercy, no, not even from God.

NOAH shoots BAYU dead.

TRAFFICKER: *(To NOAH.)* Brave Calipha! But your confusion is a fault and your enemy senses it; he's escaped into the desert.

NOAH staggers beyond the perimeter in pursuit of the MANAGER.)

CASHIER: *(Over the tannoy.)* Turn the electricity on, boy. Our Calipha needs more than the light of God to shoot straight.

The halogen floodlights warm up.

JOSEPH hangs dead from the tree.

CASHIER: Dead dog north, dead dog South. What is this, a horror flick?

TRAFFICKER: We'll take the pickup. You drive; I'll shoot.

CASHIER: Wait, I need a hat!

TRAFFICKER: What are we, colonialists? Khan, prepare Johnny Walker.

Exit CASHIER and TRAFFICKER.

The GIRL begins a song of lamentation.

SCENE FOUR

Dawn: light breaks on the horizon. The sky is clearer now, the polluting mists of clouds and oil have broken and the light of the sun is clear, proud and urgent. The GIRL is singing a lament.

KHAN: I brought you a loincloth and some water.

GIRL: You bring me life.

KHAN: It is dawn and no one to call the prayers.

GIRL: Pure dawn.

KHAN: I must bury my friends.

GIRL: Take your passport. It's in his office.

KHAN hesitates, looks around him.

GIRL: I will bury all the dead: take your passport, run.

KHAN: Thank you. Thank you, miss.

KHAN runs to the CASHIER's office.

The FATHER emerges from his cabin and walks towards the GIRL.

FATHER: You've returned?

GIRL: Yes. I –

FATHER: Let me see you.

GIRL: Yes.

FATHER: Let me hold you.

GIRL: Yes.

FATHER: I loved you so much. I disemboweled the earth in search of you.

GIRL: I came out of the blood red earth, my hands are trembling, I don't know why, I want them to stop trembling, but I don't know why –

FATHER: Give me your hands.

GIRL: Why am I so weak –

FATHER: Bring me our son.

GIRL: …and the rage of the dead so strong –

FATHER: Call him, call our son!

GIRL: …the fury of the living so vile.

FATHER: Call him, please.

GIRL: He's coming.

FATHER: Describe him to me.

GIRL: He is tall and handsome, like his father. His forehead is not creased with lies. His chest is open to the sun, he walks in great strides towards us, he is smiling, and brings me joy: he makes our love real.

FATHER: I want to die in these arms, let me kiss them and die, Maria.

(He leans his body against her and kisses her arms.)

GIRL: I came here to escape death, old man!

The FATHER falls to the ground, dead.

Enter the MANAGER carrying the dead body of NOAH onto the platform.

GIRL: Bring him to me.

MANAGER: His neck was brittle as a sapling branch. In the combat of dogs what he did not know, I could not teach him.

GIRL: Lay him down.

MANAGER: When I yoked him to my chest, I felt his wounds leak onto my body; I said, 'my brother wants me dead but you, stranger, will you carry the hatred of a brother?'

GIRL: Tell me his words.

MANAGER: He said, 'Bring her, bring her, bring my sister, she knows the meaning of words, she knows the meaning of dreams. I must speak to her, I must tell her my dream.' His neck went limp in my hands like an empty petrol hose.

(Seeing the FATHER.)

Must you be dead when I am whole?

GIRL: Bury them together. What is your name?

MANAGER: My name's Noah.

GIRL: Take this.

MANAGER: What is it?

GIRL: My brother's passport.

MANAGER: Why?

GIRL: It's all I have left: to administer the meaning of death.

MANAGER: Where will you go?

GIRL: To learn a new language, live childless till I speak it.

The GIRL mounts the truck, starts the engine and exits.

The MANAGER, hesitates, then follows.

SCENE FIVE

The CASHIER and the TRAFFICKER, bloodied, intoxicated, stumble onto the platform.

TRAFFICKER: Nice driving, nephew.

CASHIER: What do you call this a fucking disaster movie? Sky's raining petrol, the romance is choking my throat. *(Seeing the dead FATHER.)* Dead? Dead? O bliss, o blessed day, o new covenant! The old man's dead! He's dead! And someone's buried him! It's all mine, Uncle Scum, it's all mine! There's the rotten skeleton of the dead whore over there, too. Rich pickings, the fruit of a life really worth living – God I'm happy I'm me! *(Shouting.)* Now fuck off of my land, son of no man. Go on, leave quietly like the dog you were born to be. Come out of hiding! I can't shoot you – I'm out of puff. *(To the TRAFFICKER.)* Where is he?

TRAFFICKER: My truck's gone. There's no one here.

CASHIER: *(Singing.)* She loves you, yeah, yeah, yeah, she loves you yeah, yeah –

TRAFFICKER seizes CASHIER by the throat and raises him from the ground.

CASHIER: Come on Khalloo, just having some fun, Khalloo, let me go, I'll make you an offer.

(He lowers him to the ground.)

TRAFFICKER: Make me your offer.

CASHIER: Is this the moment to be smoking a cigar? Really?

TRAFFICKER: They were my honeymoon gift to myself.

CASHIER: Give me one.

TRAFFICKER offers CASHIER a cigar and lights it.

CASHIER: I don't see many options for us.

TRAFFICKER: What do you mean?

CASHIER: I mean either I give you half the station or there's some terrible crime that's taken place, or about to take place that no one could ever sanction – would you agree?

TRAFFICKER: Sounds fair to me.

CASHIER: Right. There you go, then. *(Throws the lit cigar onto a pool of petrol that ignites powerfully.)* There's your half. Go get it.

TRAFFICKER: You fucking crazy! Here, take your half, go on! *(Throws his own cigar onto another pool of petrol that ignites.)* How's that?

CASHIER: Fair! I'd say that's fair! Let's move away from the inferno, I can't think straight.

TRAFFICKER: Fucking idiot! What do we do now?

CASHIER: Dunno. Register as unemployed? It's a rentier state, you know, provision for non-productive citizens is second to none. Had enough of being an entrepreneur. I'll do fuck all for a while.

TRAFFICKER: And what about me?

CASHIER: We'll find you a mosque to preach in, day job, tide you over.

TRAFFICKER: I used to be a communist, you know.

CASHIER: Don't brag, Uncle, it's like saying I had polio, it's nothing to be proud of.

TRAFFICKER: We could join a militia.

CASHIER: Be no good: I'd kill everyone.

TRAFFICKER: Fucking hell!

CASHIER: Pump it again.

TRAFFICKER: Fucking hell.

CASHIER: Do it together, for good luck.

CASHIER & **TRAFFICKER**: Fucking hell!

***